A Nostalgia for Camels

A Nostalgia for Camels

by

CHRISTOPHER RAND

An Atlantic Monthly Press Book
Little, Brown and Company
BOSTON   TORONTO

Eight of the sketches in this book — all but "Flight to Urumchi," "The Jungle Stalker," and "A Nostalgia for Camels" — have appeared in *The New Yorker*, though in somewhat different form. I thank *The New Yorker* for its permission to republish these pieces, and for its generous support in the writing of them. Without *The New Yorker* they could not have been done.

ATLANTIC–LITTLE, BROWN BOOKS
ARE PUBLISHED BY
LITTLE, BROWN AND COMPANY
IN ASSOCIATION WITH
THE ATLANTIC MONTHLY PRESS

*Published simultaneously in Canada
by Little, Brown & Company (Canada) Limited*

PRINTED IN THE UNITED STATES OF AMERICA

Author's Note

This book was written in Asia during the past decade, a time of flux in that continent's affairs. Therefore it may be helpful for readers to know the year when each sketch was done.

"The Human Radar" was written in Singapore in 1952; "Flight to Urumchi" in 1948 — a year or two before the Communists gained control of Chinese Turkestan, changing the situation there radically; "Dunhill" in Hong Kong or Macao in 1951; "The New City" in India in 1955; "The Faqir of Ipi" in Karachi, Pakistan, in 1954; "Tenzing" in India in 1954; "Nine Hundred Mules" in 1953 (being virtually dictated to me by my brother); "A Walk with Vinoba" in India in 1955; "The Jungle Stalker" in Singapore in 1952; "Old Man River" in Ceylon in 1956; "A Nostalgia for Camels" in Hong Kong in 1953.

Innumerable friends and acquaintances have helped me with these sketches — in writing them and in getting the material. I cannot thank them separately; but they all know what they did, and I trust they know how grateful I am for it.

Contents

A Nostalgia for Camels

To my family

The Human Radar

THE PEOPLE of the Malayan east coast look seaward
more than do most Asians. They verge on the amphibi-
ous. Their side of the Malay Peninsula is backward compared to the western one, where railways have spread a
coating of plantations, mines, towns, and immigrants,
the last mainly Chinese. The Chinese on the east coast
are few, the mines and estates are scattered and lonely,
and of towns there are almost none. One can drive up the
coast for half a day, pausing now and then to ferry
across a muddy river, and see little in the human line
but Malay *kampongs* — villages of stilted wooden huts —
shaded by coco palms and fronting on the blue tropical
sea. A scheme for building a good highway up through
east Malaya is often discussed in the government, a fun-
damentally British affair that is slowly reverting to the
local people, at least in theory. In these talks, it is said,
British officials urge that the road be laid a few dozen
miles inland, to develop the country and avoid swamps

and river mouths, but their Malay colleagues tend to hold
out for the coast line, so the fishermen will get the most
gain. The coast has a hard time in the winter, when the
northeast monsoon bears on it after a full sweep down the
South China Sea. The monsoon hampers the fishing,
chews at the shoreline, and backs the rivers up into
floods — in its worst month, mid-December to mid-
January, east-coast officials may not travel without permission, for fear they will be stranded. Perhaps to
meet this harsh weather, the east-coast Malays have developed special skills. They build boats that are rated
much sounder and more durable than the west-coast
ones, and they have established particular bonds with
the water life. It is often said, for instance, that their
pawangs, or magicians, can charm crocodiles out of the
streams. These reports are widely doubted, but there is
no doubt at all that in sea fishing the Malays use what
are sometimes called "human radars" — *juru selam*, men
who go under water to identify the fish and listen for
their whereabouts and movements. This art, experts on
Malaya believe, is practiced nowhere else.

A short while ago I visited the east coast, traveling
there from Singapore, at the peninsula's tip, on a three-
hundred-twenty-ton coasting vessel of the Straits Steam-
ship Company, which handles a lot of the Malaysian
carrying trade. Our ship was suitably led in toward port
by some dolphins that came to meet us — first two, then
four, then as many as seven including a little one. They

were streaky in the morning light, liverish and grayish
like pale corroded bronze. They swam along under the
bow like ghosts, now on their bellies, now on their sides
and showing the profile of their beaks; and they sounded
and surfaced in their even wavy rhythm. Sometimes one
would swing out many yards to port or starboard, surface, and come back; but on the whole they stayed before us like a dog team. After a while they left us and
we crept on slowly, taking soundings, through shallows
containing green-brown jellyfish, acres of them, spaced
evenly and closely as if in a truck garden. We waited
among them a few hours for the tide to come in, and then
toward noon we entered a flat glaring river with a small
baking town half a mile upstream on one bank, complete
with palms, Chinese shops, and touches of corrugated
iron — the facing bank was all jungle: unbroken green
coming down into the water. We tied up to another
little freighter, with a rusty deck, that was moored there,
and we disembarked before a sleepy crowd of people and
thin dogs.

For the next few days I stayed in a house by the river,
and I walked on the bank in the early mornings. It happened to be low tide then, and brown slimy mud flats
would lie exposed between me and the water. A great
many swallows would be out, black ones with white
patches on their backs, and indeed the buildings on all
the Malayan rivers I have seen are plastered with swallows' nests, and noisy at dawn and dusk with their mew-
ing. There were several kingfishers, large and small, in

different shades of blue; some of them screeched, some worked in pairs, some flew low over the smooth water, making circles on it with their wing tips. The water was constantly broken by fish movements, especially along the edge of the mud flats — curves, swirls, swishes, splashes, reflections of pursuit. A few times I saw what I thought were crocodiles' wakes, though I wasn't sure; they were long and pointed and they usually advanced in a straight line, perhaps upstream; they moved jerkily, not like a fish but like a frog or swimmer.

I learned a bit of crocodile lore by inquiry and reading. Malayan crocodiles have been known to reach thirty feet in length and are said to be the world's biggest reptiles. They live usually in the lower stretches of rivers, but sometimes go to sea and sometimes make long trips overland. The crocodile is king of the water as the tiger is king of the jungle, and it holds a like place in the people's mind. Crocodiles and tigers are looked on as manifestations of Shiva, the "destroyer" in the Hindu mythology that once flourished on the Malay Peninsula. Crocodiles will grow fierce, the Malays say, if bad language is used on a river. There are all kinds of legends about the crocodile. It fell out with the monkey, for instance, over an attempted swindle. The crocodile's wife was sick, and the monkey's heart was prescribed as a remedy. So the crocodile swam up to the jungle's edge, found the monkey in a tree, and set out to hoodwink him. He used an approach deemed sound with monkeys in Malaya. He said his wife was sick and asked where the best doctor in the world could be found. The monkey confessed that he himself was that doctor, and the crocodile promised him a gigantic fee for coming to the sickbed. The monkey got on the crocodile's back, they swam off, and when they were away from land the crocodile revealed that it was all a dodge to get the monkey's heart. The monkey kept a straight face but thought furiously, and he quickly answered, with regret, that he had chanced to take his heart out that morning and had left it behind, hanging in a tree. The crocodile fell for this and went back, and the monkey swarmed up his tree and began jeering. Monkeys have been jeering at crocodiles ever since, disclosing their whereabouts to the jungle.

Crocodiles sometimes lapse into killing people (often by dragging them under and drowning them), and the Malays are said to feel this is wrong by natural law, much as is man-eating by tigers. This idea gets into the tradition whereby magicians charm crocodiles out of the water — they can do it only to levy punishment for killing humans, one hears, and then only under certain conditions.

I was unable to learn much about this practice, partly because of its confusion with another one — straightforward "fishing" for crocodiles with baited hooks. The Malays apparently do a good deal of the latter. A small float of bamboo is set out with a chicken or monkey resting on it, alive or dead, along with a big hook or a springstick arrangement that will catch in the crocodile's throat. Once a crocodile is hooked it is led quietly ashore —

quietly, one sometimes hears, because of incantations made in the process. But a British planter I met on the east coast said there was nothing to the incantations. He said he had once assisted at such a killing and had led the crocodile in himself; he had kept it docile just by playing it with a gentle touch on the line; charms had not entered in — the whole Malay notion of charms, indeed, was plain superstition.

On the other hand the planter may have missed some sides of crocodile handling. A Malay servant in the house where I stayed told how he had once seen a magician bring a crocodile onto the bank entirely by occult means, without using hook, line, or any other paraphernalia. The magician had gone to the water's edge and had blown softly three times. The crocodile had risen to the surface, and the magician had beckoned him ashore — the servant, in explaining this, backed up softly and beckoned slowly with his right hand down by his knees. Once ashore the crocodile had been cut open, with a *parang*, or long Malay knife, by the younger brother of the Sultan, and the bones of six people had been found inside it. There had been a hundred witnesses, the servant said.

I also heard that magicians talked to the crocodiles they worked on, asking them if they would submit to coming ashore, and generally trying to impose their will on them; I heard of crocodiles' being induced even to climb high, steep banks in this way. That was as far as I got, though, despite a good deal of help from the local officials. It happened that a child had been carried off in that river about a month before my visit, and the officials had sent a magician after the offending crocodile. The magician had failed to raise it, though according to his claims he had made good on twenty previous jobs. He had said he thought someone had shot at the crocodile between the child's death and his appearance in the case, and this had made it less open to punishment. Crocodiles can't be put in jeopardy, it seems, by gunners and magicians as well.

I had better luck with the "human radar" side of east-coast life. The district officer of the section arranged for me to go out one day on a fishing boat, in company with the fisheries inspector for that part of the coast, a Malay named Che (or Mr.) Osman. I spent the night before in a *kampong* by the beach, where the waves fell softly and the wind rustled in the palm trees. It was the start of Ramadan, the fasting lunar month of the Malays, who are Muslims — the evening moon was still no more than a sliver. I rose before dawn and was met by Che Osman, who turned out to be a smiling, pleasant, thick-set man. We had to wait awhile for the fishermen; perhaps their timing had been thrown off by the fasting; the Malays eat only by dark during Ramadan; their last meal is usu-ally at 3 A.M., and they try to follow it with a nap, a regime I suppose may be hard, each year, to shift into.

It was strong daylight when we finally started, crossing the wet gray sand and climbing into a long boat, after removing our shoes to avoid bad luck.

The boat was long and narrow and there were sixteen men in it, including two boys of around twelve; most of them rowed at the start as it was nearly dead calm. With few exceptions they wore sarongs; these were of all patterns, flowered or striped, and they were mostly faded, though a new orange one in a nearby boat stood out like flame. The men had other sarongs tied round their heads or necks, and Che Osman said it was usual to take a spare, even if you didn't plan to go in the water and wet the first one. Some men wore sun hats made of palm leaves — trim cones in simple colors — green, blood red, robin's-egg blue. Men and gear were crowded in the narrow space. Piles of brown fish-smelling net lay on the bottom, with stones like eggplants tied on for weights, and bamboo sticks for floats. A small boat, perhaps eight feet long, was stuck in amidships. The main boat's sides were white with green trimmings. The sails lay on crutches carved from plank in baroque whirls, and the lines of the bow and stern were carried onward, into the air, with simple decorative timbers longer than a man. They gave a gondola effect.

Che Osman said the design of east-coast boats was slipping. "Five years ago they had nice figureheads," he said. "Now people just want boats that can be built easily. No more decoration; it is fast changing." He spoke softly and directly and smiled a good deal. "If the models of these boats aren't kept now," he said, "I think they will disappear in fifteen or twenty years."

We drew away from land, and the green jungled hills behind us turned bluer. We felt a breeze and raised the sail; it was square, in strips of dirty whites and grays. The rowing stopped, there was less movement and more room, and Che Osman and I settled in the stern.

The fishermen were poor, Che Osman said. Most were in debt to *towkays*, rich Chinese. They borrowed from the Chinese, especially in the monsoon; they sold their catch to them cheap and bought goods from them dear. Many boats were owned by Chinese too. A Malay started fishing at about twelve years; normally he reached his peak at thirty, when if he was gifted he would hold a key job in a boat such as the one we were in; after that he would decline unless he had learned some special skill, like that of a *juru selam*; by forty he might be out of the big boats and doing small odds and ends, and he could look forward to a poor old age. In a village like the one we had come from, Che Osman said, perhaps only two or three men in three hundred would own land. A good deal of the fishermen's income was spent in coffee shops. "Whenever a village gets prosperous more coffee shops spring up there. It is too bad. There isn't much thought of the future."

Che Osman had been with the fisheries for sixteen years, after trying the police and the clerical service, which he hadn't liked. His father had advised him against the police, he said, on the grounds that interfering with

others was against the Malay nature. His fisheries work
entailed constant travel on the coast, much of it by foot,
and constant mixing with fishermen. When he was a boy
his father had been a fisherman himself awhile, in this
same region, and Che Osman thought it would be good if
all fisheries inspectors came from fishing families. Most
came now from the white-collar class, whose approach
to the fishing life tended to be abstract. One could see
that Che Osman got on well with fishermen. I thought
he belonged to a type fairly common in modern Asia —
the young practical idealist who has identified himself
with a segment of the poor and is working to improve its
lot, not much deterred by the political upheavals around
him.

The boat we were in was a *perahu payang*, he said,
perahu meaning boat, *payang* being the type. The small
boat amidships, which would be used by the *juru selam*,
was an *anak payang*, or "*payang*'s child." The *juru selam*
was sitting near us; he was a thin, tired-looking man of
about sixty, toothless, dressed in a white cotton singlet
with many holes and a coffee sarong with pink-and-
white flowers, all faded; his extra sarong, faded too, was
in a green-and-white plaid design. He seemed less impressive than the next highest personage aboard, the *juru
solo*, his assistant, apprentice, and understudy, who was
a younger man and, as it turned out, the owner of the
boat. The *juru solo* sat on the gunwale ahead of us,
directing the oarsmen and paddling with a Malay paddle
— they have short handles and long pointed blades. He

was well set up, slight but with broad shoulders; his muscles were hard and his hips very narrow. He wore a pale-green cone hat, a gray singlet, and a sky-blue sarong, and his extra sarong, tied round his neck like a scarf, was dull black with a white line pattern. Che Osman pointed out other specialists: the helmsman; a man who handled the bulk of the net; one who stayed in the bow and gave directions as the net was lowered; and one who bailed the boat, looked after it when ashore, cleaned it, and gathered the crew in the morning. All the rest, men and boys, were ordinary hands and got ordinary shares of the catch.

The *juru selam* told us he didn't come from this village, but from a place some distance up the coast. He had been called here this year to run things for the Number Two, the owner, who I gathered had not learned enough to manage by himself. The old man had been a *juru selam* for fifteen years. You could learn the art in two years of arduous apprenticeship, he said, but you might need as many as five if you took it easy. He had been taught by his father, who had been a *juru selam* too. That was the old custom: passing the knowledge from father to son, keeping it in the family — if there was no son the father had customarily adopted an apprentice.

Now it was different, the old man said, and nearly anyone could come up from the ranks if he worked hard enough. After a while he fell silent. His skin was wrinkled and burned to the shade of a coffee bean. He was thin and quiet and had a mournful, faraway look.

We sailed gently across the south wind. A single gull flew past — there were not many birds around. Sultry thunderhead clouds lined the horizon. At length the *juru selam* rose, looked about him, and ordered the small boat lowered. Along with the Number Two he stepped into it, carrying a wooden box on a shoulder cord, which Che Osman said held betel-nut makings. He also took half a coconut shell for bailing. The boat had almost no freeboard when the men were in it. It went away fast, both of them paddling vigorously with their long paddles.

"There is one thing about the old man," Che Osman said. "When he is in the big boat he looks a frail figure. But once in the little boat he is strong. I have seen this many times. When they are in the big boat they are lifeless — is that how you say it? But when they are out they are strong."

A few score yards away the small boat stopped, and the Number Two climbed deftly into the water from the bow. He went under the surface, and all you could see of him was a brown arm and hand reaching to the gunwale. Then he reappeared and climbed back in again, his singlet and sarong dripping, and they paddled on.

"Not a sign of fish," Che Osman said.

The pair worked away from us, off the starboard bow, and after a while the Number Two went down again — down, up for air, down, up. Again he pulled himself into the bow, and again they were off.

I had noticed high plumes of water, like spray, coming from the little boat, and now I discovered that these were made by the *juru selam*, bailing quickly. He was wearing a cream-colored conical sun hat that I hadn't seen before.

The Number Two went over again and submerged, but still no sign of fish.

Soon they were working hundreds of yards away to starboard, which was also to windward. We just waited. The men rowed the big boat awhile to shorten the gap. I lost track of how many times the little boat stopped and the Number Two went overboard — the *juru selam* himself was doing none of this yet. The little boat was so far away one could not watch it sharply. The easiest thing to see was the quick white plumes of the bailing.

Some other boats were near by, off our stern, and in time we could see from their behavior that they were finding fish. Our steersman called out to the small boat, and it started back to us. It came slowly, taking it easy, having already ranged far and fast upwind, to no avail. The two men looked exercised, but still "strong," as they passed us. They went on downwind and we followed, raising a small sail that was nearly square like the big one.

The Number Two went over again, and when his head came up the *juru selam* raised his paddle high in the air. Fish had been found. A cry went up from our boat, and the men started rowing eagerly to the spot, shouting to keep time.

The *juru selam* himself was down in the water now, getting further information, and the Number Two was in the small boat. He guided our movements with arm signals. When we drew near him the crew began laying the net, tossing it overboard along with its stones and bamboos, rowing quickly, shouting, and watching the signals. The net was laid in a circle, enclosing the small boat, and when we got back to the starting end the crew anchored at once and began hauling in, shouting all the time — no joint effort could be made, it seemed, without the shouting.

The small boat had gone to the far end of the net — the business end with the fine mesh that would do the catching — and the *juru selam* was in the water, listening and relaying instructions through the Number Two.

Soon the Number Two slapped his paddle on the surface and the two small boys of the crew, who had taken up posts amidships on the net-side gunwale, thrust poles into the water and began beating them loudly with sticks. "It is to frighten the fish so they won't escape," Che Osman said. He said it was effective, though later in the day he showed me poles in other boats that were still better; they had rings of wire fixed near their ends, with sea shells strung on these, a rig that he said put out a fearful din when under water.

The boys beat the poles, working up a fancy rhythm; the men hauled and shouted; the *juru selam* stayed in the water, putting his head under to listen or raising it with dripping face. In time the catch was brought to the top — mainly small flat silver fish called *lelemah*.

The crew members, standing by, began picking fish out one by one for their shares, according to a system I didn't make out, and the *juru selam* paddled up to join in. I thought he looked purposeful now rather than mournful. When the picking was done the bulk of the catch was stowed under the floor boards, and a new operation began, the small boat darting off, the Number Two going overboard again.

By this time other big boats were laying nets on either side of us, directed by their small ones. "Fishermen are like birds," Che Osman said. "They flock together when fish are plentiful, then separate when they are gone." The boats made a racket with their shouting and beating on poles as they laid their nets or hauled them in. It was like a playing field with many games in progress. The glare was bright, and all around were blue tones – blue sky, blue water, blue clouds, blue smell of the sunny air. The distant hills on shore were a real blue now, though the strip of palms was green below them on the beach.

The second catch was made up chiefly of a small fish called *beliak mata* – "big eyes." There were other kinds mixed in. One of the crew picked out a long fish, like a small pickerel, and put it on a hook which he dropped overboard on a hand line. A few single fishermen were working near by, trolling from little sailboats, and one of them came alongside us and got a few fish for bait – I don't know whether he was given them or bought them on credit.

On the third try the *juru selam* headed away from the other boats. He seemed to be stalking a shoal of fish. He would get down, listen, get back into the boat and paddle off with the Number Two on a new tack, beckoning us to follow. Then he would do it again. Che Osman said that a seasoned *juru selam*, like this one, was good not only at finding fish, and identifying them, but at sensing their direction. The work had a dimension of motion and timing to it. Che Osman said it was like bird shooting, which happened to be his hobby.

The third catch was mainly of pomfret, a valuable fish. By the fourth try I realized that what I was watching was really a roundup, like a roundup of animals. The *juru selam* located a shoal of fish, kept after it, and had the big boat lay the net round it as quickly as it could — the net made a circle about fifty yards in diameter. While the net was being hauled in he continued to follow the shoal's actions, and he ordered the procedure modified to suit these. He called for the pole-beating noise when it seemed the fish might break out through the net's open, boatward end. The *juru selam* and his assistant were the brains of the operation. They made all the decisions, and the big boat merely followed their orders, whether promptly or not. I figured that each of them did twice as much work as anyone else.

The fourth catch was mainly of *kerong-kerong*, a small striped fish that isn't worth much but that often has pomfret swimming with it, which Che Osman said was why the *juru selam* had chosen this shoal. The fish made a noise even after they were caught. They were put under the floor boards and soon a deep humming rose from there, as of a great many bees or flies. I was puzzled by it at first, and looked for a wind in the rigging to account for it.

It was noon now, and the sun beat down from the blue sky. There was neither food nor drink aboard, because of the fasting. The crew, especially the young boys, began turning to horseplay, roughhousing and throwing each other's things in the water. They rowed more slowly when laying the net the fifth time. The old *juru selam* grumbled at them, and from the water made quick imperative gestures with his dripping arm; yet they hauled the net in lackadaisically, and the boys beat faintly on the poles. The catch was small this time — Che Osman said the fishing had been bad lately because the water was too clear. Soon the sail was raised, the Number Two came aboard and began going through the catch, and we started homeward, towing the *juru selam*, who sat hunched in the small boat, resting in the breeze.

I don't think "human radar" is a good phrase for describing a *juru selam*, though it is a natural one for Westerners, who view the matter from the outside, from the machine age. The art is really based on the development of primitive senses to an exceptional degree, together, or so it is believed, with a touch of the supernatural. The senses used are chiefly hearing and sight. There seems no evidence that smell gets into it, though the Malays are said to be good at smelling crocodiles on the rivers. The underwater hearing of these fishermen may be un-

equaled among humans anywhere. An Englishman on
the east coast who has a boat with a loud exhaust says
they can hear it eighteen miles away under water —
long before they can see it, or hear it through the air.

After we came in that day we had a chance to talk
with the *juru selam*, under a shady roof among the coconut palms. He sat in a straight chair, looking out to sea,
and described his procedure. When he went under, he
said, he first looked in all directions, and if he saw a dark
or cloudy spot he climbed back into the boat, went there
at once, submerged again, and began listening. If he
heard fish it meant they were somewhere near by on the
sea bed, and from the sound he would figure out where,
and he would go there and stay over them till they were
netted. On this part of the coast the fishermen usually
worked at the eleven-fathom line, he said, but in the part
where he had come from they went as deep as thirty-
five fathoms. This took longer, but the fish were more
plentiful there, and a boat had to lay its net only a couple
of times in a day, as against the five or six needed here.
Another difference was that shoals of fish were pure in
the waters he had come from, without odd varieties
mixed in, whereas here they were jumbled, and harder
to identify.

He said he told the fish apart chiefly by the kind of
noise they made in their throats — "clucking" or "grunt-
ing" was how Che Osman expressed it in English. The
lelemah was loudest, the *juru selam* said, and made a
noise somewhat like "*kha, kha.*" One fish whose name

I didn't catch said "*ah . . . oh . . . ah*" — the sounds
were nasal and well separated — when it was alone, but
something more like "*ump . . . ump*" when swimming
in a shoal. Another fish said "*gho-ho-ho-oow.*" *Beliak
mata* — big eyes — made a sound like "*tikatikatikatika-
socosocosoco*" — the old man whispered this softly, as if
to himself, and turned his head back and forth while
doing so. Some fish, he said, sounded like approaching
wind. When a few fish were heard clucking, it usually
meant there were a good many in that spot, but when
many were heard it meant they were scattering and the
shoal would be sparse. Predicting the movements of fish
was largely a matter of knowledge and experience. There
was one kind that always swam against the tide or current, but most followed it. There was nearly always a
current of some sort along this coast, and familiarity
with it, of course, was part of the game. Indeed it seems
that the sense of touch, for feeling currents and winds,
must be well developed in a *juru selam* along with those
of sight and hearing, though this man didn't say so.

I asked about sharks, and he said there were none
around at this time of year, and they weren't much of a
problem anyway. If a shark was aroused you could hear
it far away, making a noise like "*snnnnnng KWAH.*"
But it was rare for sharks to get angry at humans, and
besides you could always see them easily in the water.

"I believe these men think they have learning that can
shield them from big fish," Che Osman said, and indeed
one hears from all sides that religion and magic play a

great part in a *juru selam*'s affairs. His skill is thought of as skill in ritual, one hears, rather than in pure technique. If he does well it is by the bounty of God, and perhaps also the bounty of demons. It is usual for a *juru selam* to pray to Allah before going under water, and to think of Allah while there — otherwise he can't expect good results.

On this point, of course, the whole practice is opposed to modern times, though not on this point alone. Spending from two to five years in learning a primitive hunter's skill is hardly in the twentieth-century style. Che Osman and the *juru selam* had a discussion that day about the future. The *juru selam* thought the art would survive, but Che Osman was doubtful. "Before long these boats will be motorized," he said to me, "at least with outboard motors, and then people will lose interest in the old methods."

The way things are going in Asia, one can hardly doubt that Che Osman is right. If he is, we can expect the Malayan east coast to be more like every other place before long. Then we may see no more of humans who can hear fish noises, or who even know there are such things. We may hear no more accounts of crocodile charming. In general, we shall all be farther up the bank and out of the water, if that is what we want.

Flight to Urumchi

IN 1947 I had occasion to fly from Shanghai, on the Westernized China coast, to Urumchi, capital of the Central Asian province of Chinese Turkestan, about two thousand miles away. The flight took mail and some officials to Urumchi, a place that could formerly be reached only by weeks of desert travel, and it showed how the airplane has tightened political and economic control over such faraway places. But it showed too that a good deal of wear and tear has accompanied this change. Our trip lasted two days, and it was a constant, if subdued, struggle between the East, represented by the passengers, and the West, represented by the plane and its pilot, a blue-eyed young Englishman named Dick Foote, who had been put on this difficult run because he was good and was known to be strict about procedures.

The trouble began at the outset, when the plane was being loaded in Shanghai. It was an American C-46 belonging to the Central Air Transport Corporation, a

Chinese Government passenger line, and like many CATC ships was still fitted with "bucket seats," the primitive canvas slings that had been used during the war. When Foote came aboard he found a deck chair sitting prominently in the fuselage, surrounded by the bucket seats and by some freight. The chair struck a bad note. It indicated that special arrangements were being made for some passenger — that the flight might involve a personal problem aside from its mechanical ones. Foote turned to the Chinese chief of the ground crew, the only man who could have been responsible for the chair's presence, and asked him about it.

"It is for a sick person who will board the plane at Nanking," was the answer. Nanking, China's capital, was to be our first stop, about an hour distant.

Foote frowned in a way that clearly made the ground-crew chief uneasy. (I discovered later that Foote was described by the Chinese who worked with him as *ch'i-kuai* — "strange," or even "violent and unaccountable" — at any rate, someone who should be propitiated.) "But we can't take sick people," he said. "If we get lost in the mountains we will have to fly very high, and we have no oxygen."

"It isn't a sick person exactly, but a very old person."

"Well, that's no better. How old?"

The chief laughed in an embarrassed way. "More than thirty-five," he said. Foote apparently decided he was getting nowhere. He went forward to the cockpit, and pretty soon we took off.

When we reached Nanking it turned out that the chair had been put in — in answer to someone's long-range instructions — for Madame Wang Mo-an, the wife of a high official in Chinese Turkestan, who was going up with us to join her husband. She was waiting when we taxied up to our berth, and was surrounded by an impressive retinue that had come to see her off. Among others this included two generals, one with three stars, and a number of women dressed in the luxurious, cosmopolitan, silky fashion of the more modern Chinese cities. There were three shiny black automobiles behind the group, and it all sparkled brightly on the green grass under the morning sun. Madame Wang herself was neither old nor infirm, it turned out, but young, strong, attractive and dressed to kill, with black suède shoes, nylon stockings, a gray suit, and lively red lipstick on a generous mouth. While we were refueling she managed, with the help of the generals, to put aboard perhaps three hundred pounds of "hand baggage," including suitcases, bundles and several of the baskets of fruit, cans of tea and small pots of condiments, each bearing a message on red paper, that polite Chinese must take to their friends when they travel. Foote watched this with obvious disapproval, but he did nothing about it. He was again busy jacking up the ground crew, this time because the gas hadn't materialized quickly enough.

After Nanking things were pretty well settled in the plane, because we had our final load on. We were carrying mail and about twenty cases of light cargo. Besides

myself we had nine passengers, all Chinese members of
the Turkestan bureaucracy — officials, army officers and
the wife of one of the latter, a Mrs. Liu, who except for
Madame Wang was the only woman aboard. The Na-
tionalist Chinese government subsidized the flights to
Turkestan, which was next to Russia and was partly in
revolt, in order to keep in close touch with its bureaucracy there. Our load of officials and mail represented a
quick transfusion to this bureaucracy. I watched the
other passengers as we flew along, and was interested to
see how quickly they began adapting themselves to the
Turkestan official hierarchy, which some of them had
never seen before, but which they were speeding through
the air to join. Madame Wang, who by the standards of
that hierarchy was the most important personage in our
midst, became simply the queen of the plane — or at
least of the section reserved for passengers. Foote had
objected to the deck chair partly because it meant that
one individual was to get special treatment through pull
of some sort — that fair play was not being observed on
his ship. Except as a matter of abstract principle he
needn't have worried. The other passengers had no objection to Madame Wang's chair, unless they may have
thought it wasn't grand enough. They gathered round
and helped her with blankets and cushions, coming forward when she needed something, withdrawing defer-
entially when she didn't. Mrs. Liu became a maid in
waiting, as plainly so labeled as if she had worn livery.
Chinese travelers carry thermos bottles when possible,

so they can drink boiled water or tea. Madame Wang had
one of these, and Mrs. Liu automatically took charge
of it, filling it at every opportunity and keeping it handy
for her mistress's use. She rummaged through Madame
Wang's bags when a handkerchief or sweater was needed.
These and other small attentions, though rendered in a
menial way, were in keeping with the old Chinese official style and had none of the bad grace that would have
spoiled them in America. I talked briefly from time to
time with Madame Wang, whose English, though halt-
ing, was good enough for simple subjects. She had never
been to Turkestan before. Like most Chinese she thought
of it as a remote and desolate spot, and she had misgiv-
ings about how she would enjoy the life there. As she
spoke of these and of her husband, whom she hadn't seen
for a year, she seemed thoroughly warm, open and un-
affected.

Shortly after noon we reached Sian, a large city on our
way. We should have hurried along from there, but we
couldn't do this without radio instructions from Shanghai. These failed to come through because of some mix-
up in the CATC network, which brought further impatient remarks from Foote, and we ended by spending
the night in town. Madame Wang's status didn't change
on this occasion. She and Mrs. Liu drove to the hotel in
the first car available while the others, including Mrs.
Liu's husband, waited respectfully on the field for something else.

Foote and I shared a room that night in the Sian Guest House, and I had a good chance to talk with him. He was in his late twenties and extremely good-looking in an English way, with sandy hair, a fair skin and regular features. Though affable he was grave and quiet, without the flamboyance of American pilots overseas. He discussed the state of the British Empire in a well-informed, well-organized way. He had some newspapers with him and a copy of *Brideshead Revisited,* and when we got to our room he ordered a pot of tea and settled down to read. He said he usually passed the time this way when lying over in strange cities, except when he happened to be in Lanchow, a few hundred miles to the west, a place he liked especially because he had discovered some British missionaries there who had a radio and who served homemade strawberry jam. He had been an RAF pilot during the war. After that he had flown commercially in India for a while and then had come to China because of higher pay. He belonged to a special class in postwar Chinese life — the foreign pilots, most of them Americans, whom the Chinese airlines consider indispensable. They are so considered partly because they have had good mechanical training since childhood, but even more because they are outside the Chinese social system and are better able to resist it. Not only do they demand relatively smart performance from ground crews, radio operators and so forth, but they can stand up to generals and high officials who are unschooled in machine-age disciplines, and who will ruinously delay, overload or otherwise tamper with planes when given the chance. Foote was particular about how things were done, irrespective of persons. I believe it was this, rather than any inner personal trait, that made the Chinese call him *ch'i-kuai*, or strange. By and large, indeed, he conducted himself tactfully, with the good manners that the British so often show in foreign countries.

The next morning he let me ride in the cockpit for some time, while his Chinese copilot rested in back, and I got a good view of the country and was able to talk with him about it. It was a rough and mountainous region, like the American West. It was also badly mapped. Foote pointed out one peak that rose fourteen thousand feet high, square in our path. His best chart had originally shown nothing over six thousand in that neighborhood, though he had sketched in the fourteen-thousand-footer himself. He had made the trip several times by now, and had scribbled all kinds of information on his chart — it was perhaps the best one of the area in existence.

We were now getting into the wilder and more remote parts of China, and Foote had many things to worry about. Not only were the maps unreliable, but he had to calculate his gasoline carefully. The main airfields were far apart, and little was known about in-between emergency ones, where they existed at all, except that they were poor. He had also to be especially careful of his landings and take-offs from now on. There were no repair facilities in this part of the world, and if something broke he would have to wait until equipment could be flown from Shanghai to fix it. Right now, this morning, he had an additional problem. The radio reported a sandstorm in Urumchi, and he must do everything possible to reach there before sunset. This wouldn't be easy because the layover in Sian had put us behind schedule.

Shortly after noon we landed for gas at a primitive little field near Suchow, a mountain town on the old silk route that had run across Central Asia even in Marco Polo's day, between China and the Mediterranean. The field consisted of little more than the flat gravel plain of a river that was now dry, but that in the spring would wash over the whole thing. It was sprinkled with cobblestones, and our landing was bumpy.

Foote said it would take some time to gas up, and that meanwhile we could go into Suchow for lunch. Everyone was pleased to hear this except for Madame Wang, to whom it made no difference, because at that moment a general appeared in a jeep to welcome her, having been alerted by radio, perhaps days earlier. The general insisted that she come to his headquarters, and they started off together, Foote telling Madame Wang very pointedly that she must be back in an hour. The rest of us climbed into the ramshackle old airfield truck and bumped into town. We bolted down a very good lunch at a restaurant there and hurried back again, arriving while the refueling process, a lengthy business involving hand pumps and coolie-hauled gas drums, was still going on. There was no sign of Madame Wang.

There was still no sign of her when the refueling was over and Foote had made his mechanical checks on the plane. He looked at his watch and climbed aboard, followed somewhat reluctantly by his Chinese copilot and radio operator. The passengers stayed on the ground in a small group, talking.

After a few minutes the copilot, on behalf of Foote, who didn't speak much Chinese, came to the door and ordered them aboard.

First there was a pause, and then one passenger remarked that Madame Wang was still missing.

"Captain Foote says we will start without her," said the copilot, looking as if he wished he were somewhere else. "We are supposed to stop here for only an hour, and already it is much more."

"But Madame Wang doesn't know it's supposed to be an hour," the passenger replied. "Somebody should have told her."

The copilot answered that it had all been explained to her clearly, which indeed the passenger knew anyway, since he had been standing close by when the conversation took place.

At this point the Chinese station master of the Suchow field stepped in diplomatically. He suggested that Madame Wang might be already on her way, and that a phone call should be made to the general's headquarters where she was lunching. He ordered a man to go do this. I don't know whether any call was actually made, or indeed whether there was a telephone at the field at all, but soon the messenger came back to report that Madame Wang had started and could be expected shortly.

The other passengers relaxed in their huddle near the plane, and I climbed aboard to talk with Foote, who was studying his charts in a resigned way. I described to him the scene at the general's headquarters as I imagined it, going on past experience of Chinese hospitality. The setting of this scene was primitive, in line with its outpost character — a smallish room with rough plaster walls and a simple board floor. In the center was a round table, the general on one side, Madame Wang opposite him, and a few other guests, local officials and their wives, around the sides between. Every once in a while an orderly would appear with a new dish, which he put in the center of the table. The dishes were elaborately prepared, many of them consisting of things like shark's fins and cuttlefish that had been brought from the coast at great effort. From time to time the general disparaged them and apologized to Madame Wang, explaining that Suchow was a poor place, and that no fit refreshment could be found there for her. Madame Wang for her part nibbled at each dish appreciatively, exclaiming at its excellence, and repeatedly marveling that the general had been able to create such a feast in this distant spot.

"When mushrooms are brought here they lose their flavor," I quoted the general as saying. "My cook has tried to find a way of stopping this, but so far has failed."

"I think all the flavor goes into the soup," Madame

Wang replied. "It is better than any you can get in Shanghai."

The two main actors in my scene were trapped in time-honored roles that couldn't be avoided, or changed, or speeded up. The general had to insist that Madame Wang relax thoroughly, and make his home her own as long as she cared to. In return she had to show delight, and reluctance ever to leave. The ritual, symbolic of the warmest human feelings, had been worked out ages ago, when sedan chairs and horses could wait indefinitely for the actors to leave the stage. Nowhere in it was there room for things so cold or precise as timepieces and planes.

Foote wasn't particularly amused by all this talk of mine, but he agreed that the situation must be as described, and we settled down to discuss the local geography in a distracted way. After a while, through the window, we saw the jeep speeding onto the field, and soon Madame Wang climbed breathlessly aboard, apologizing to all concerned, and followed by the other passengers in a rigid order of precedence that had been worked out early in the trip. We had one more way stop that afternoon, during which the good manners of both Foote and Madame Wang came into play. They might have parted with the feeling that one was a spoiled, troublesome woman and the other a bumptious chauffeur. But instead they talked for a while and got on such good terms that Madame Wang later rode in the cockpit, enjoying a preview of her new homeland.

The sandstorm also let up, and we made Urumchi about dusk without trouble. We flew in over the mud-walled city, looking down on camel caravans, flocks of sheep and other non-machine-age sights in the gathering darkness. A large crowd met the plane, including Madame Wang's husband and a big entourage with him. In the general air of celebration and welcome the frictions of the journey seemed to be forgotten — survived only by wonder at this Western trick that had nearly eliminated distances. It seemed as if this too might soon be forgotten, as people went about their business in the ancient city. Forgotten, that is, by everyone except Foote, the only person there who had much idea of how the trick worked, and the man who had to turn round next morning and do the whole thing over again, crossing the unmapped mountains, landing on the bumpy fields, arguing with the ground crews, and trying to hold firm against the mysteries of Chinese life.

Dunhill

LIKE NEARLY everyone, I suppose, I have long wanted to find out more about opium and opium dens, and a short while ago I had my wish through the help of a Chinese friend, Mr. J. L. Fu, who took me to a divan, as such places are called in these parts, and explained the proceedings there. Besides being an occasional smoker, Mr. Fu is an English university graduate and a master of the English language. He is a slight, retiring man of about fifty, gentle in manner and so soft spoken you could almost say he murmurs. He murmurs with intensity, though, when he says something he thinks important, such as that "it was damn poor form of Henry James to construct those sentences," or that the British habit of using different tenses is an affectation; he is firm as a rock on this point, which will strike Western readers as odd; maybe it is because the Chinese have gotten along without tenses for two thousand years. His own writing in English is simple and rhythmical, technically much bet-

ter, so far as I can tell, than most things currently published in Great Britain and America. This is not to say
he is Westernized, though; he has a Chinese way of using
aesthetic approaches to questions under discussion, rather
than purely logical ones; he sets store by the feel of
things, or the sound of the words they are expressed in.
Once an athlete of note, he is now a recluse and something of an eccentric. He seldom goes out more than
once or twice a month; he spends his time in an old high-
ceilinged octagonal room, its plaster walls discolored to
reds and grays, which houses an untamed sea of reading
matter flowing about on tables, bed and floor. He has no
timepiece that runs, and if you want to know the hour
when visiting him he bids a servant look through opera
glasses at a tower clock a mile away. This style of life
seems to mix well with opium smoking, which is a
thoughtful, unhurried activity.

Opium is a touchy subject these days, though it wasn't
always, and I cannot place the divan we visited beyond
saying it was in a city of Chinese population belonging
to one of the European empires. We were taken there
by a procurer named Ah Ling, whom we met by Mr.
Fu's arrangement on a street corner in the evening;
Mr. Fu had sent me a discreet note saying he would
introduce me to a man I should know. Ah Ling was a
Chinese of undecipherable age, and of a glib, darting and
quite ingratiating cast of face and speech. He was dressed
in a black quilted cotton winter suit, Chinese cloth shoes,

and a new-looking pearl-gray fedora, cocked back on his head. He had a short talk with Mr. Fu in Cantonese and then started down the street, we following at a distance. Ah Ling moved fast but inconspicuously; he seemed to be on wheels rather than feet; he could disappear in a crowd of two people; when he looked back to check on us he seemed not to be looking at all, but dealing with a crick in his neck; he was the innocent bystander, every inch. We left the main street we were traveling and wandered awhile in dark crooked alleys, till Ah Ling dropped back and told us to wait in a wall angle that happened to be there. As we waited I remarked to myself that the nights were getting chilly with the fall, a thing that occurs even on the edge of the tropics. Ah Ling floated up the street and into a doorway; soon he came out again and beckoned us there. He led us up a flight of steep stairs pressed in by wooden walls, and a door with a wicket opened before us; it was closed again quickly by a Chinese porter when we had entered.

We were in a wide plain room that had deep benches — six feet deep, I should say — round the walls; these were divided into stalls by token partitions a few inches high, and in each stall some coolie-class Chinese, two or more of them, lay smoking and relaxing. It seemed a full house. At the room's far end was a real partition, with a doorway, and we were led there now by a squat man who welcomed us. We found ourselves in a small place containing two facing alcoves, each with a square bench large enough for one party. It was dark there; the only light, except that from a small lamp in one alcove, came from the big room, either over the partition or through some slits in it, which seemed to have been cut for the purpose. Mr. Fu, Ah Ling and the squat man had been talking away in Cantonese, and now we were told to settle ourselves in the left-hand alcove, the other being occupied. This was a matter of taking our shoes off, getting on the bench, and disposing ourselves in a ring round the edge. I lay at the far end, against one outer wall, with Ah Ling at my feet, against the other, and Mr. Fu next my head, against the partition. We left the lip of the bench, the side that gave to the outer world, unoccupied. We fitted comfortably, with a slight curling up, and later I noticed groups of even five smokers disposed in a like space without awkwardness. Mr. Fu and I had our heads together, propped on what must be called pillows for lack of another word. They were porcelain blocks, with a thick green glaze, about six inches high and almost cube-shaped, except that their tops were cast on a bias to take the head. They were a great convenience, and in line with Southern Chinese taste, which has almost no objection to hard surfaces pressing on the body. The bench itself was hard too, of course: wood covered only by a dark-brown matting of bamboo slats, deeply polished. We settled in cozily there while a low conversation in the facing alcove went on unbroken.

Right away a servant, rather poorly dressed, brought a tray of paraphernalia and set it between us, in the middle of the bench. There was a small glass-chimneyed lamp; a pipe consisting of a straight thick wooden stem about eighteen inches long with a bowl, about the shape and size of a doorknob, fixed to its side near one end; two steel spindles, or needles, about six inches long; two tiny cylindrical containers, perhaps half an inch high, made of horn; a small pair of scissors; and a white china teapot no bigger than an apple that was presently discovered to contain oil. Cups of tea were also brought. Mr. Fu pressed me to smoke, but I demurred (wanting, on this occasion, to get the experience through his words, rather than directly). In the end he said he would have a pipe himself. "Ah Ling will make it for me," he said. "I will be what is called a one-armed smoker. That isn't quite right. A one-armed smoker doesn't know how to make pipes at all. I know how; I'm just lazy. Often in the old days the rich one-armed smokers would send for singsong girls to make for them. They wouldn't want them to do anything else; just sit there, make pipes and look beautiful."

Ah Ling touched a match to the lamp. The flame, straight and orange-colored, rose to the opening of the chimney and cast a warm glow on us. He opened one of the little horn containers and showed it to me. Inside was a brown gummy stuff, like some kind of mud or tobacco juice — a real brown, not grayish brown or reddish brown or anything like that. It didn't quite flow when I tipped the cylinder, though it looked as if it might. Ah Ling dipped the sharp point of a spindle in the gum and took it out with a drop stuck there. He held this over the flame; it swelled and bubbled and sizzled. Then he began rolling it on the lamp chimney, twirling the spindle quickly between thumb and forefinger. He dipped it into the horn container again and got more opium. He rolled some more. The opium seemed to behave like rubber cement. He rolled it on the pipe bowl awhile (bowl isn't an ideal word for this object, which was domed over like a doorknob except for a small shallow conical depression in the middle with a pinhole in its bottom; except for this it was convex, not concave). Ah Ling kept adding opium and rolling it till he had a pill the size of a big caviar egg. I asked Mr. Fu what the ritual accomplished.

"It solidifies the opium," he said, "though not in the sense of making it brittle. I think cook is the best word. It transforms the opium to a solid much as you transform an egg when you cook it." He took the spindle from Ah Ling and let me feel the pill. It was hot and quite firm; I could barely press it out of shape by squeezing hard. It made a dull clink when I tapped it on the lamp chimney.

Ah Ling took the pill back, worked it some more, and then thrust it, with the spindle, into the depression of the bowl's center. He held it there a moment and drew the spindle out. The pill was left stuck in the depression, a hole in its middle where the spindle had been, and this connecting with the pinhole in the depression's bottom. He handed the pipe to Mr. Fu, who put his lips to the mouthpiece — not around it, but against it; mouthpiece and stem were about an inch in diameter. Ah Ling had kept hold of the stem's other end, and now he maneuvered the pipe, holding it upside down, till the pill was over the flame. Mr. Fu inhaled, continuously, deeply, in a long breath. The pill again sizzled and seethed, its noise turned to a hiss or small roar by the duration in time. Dense white smoke issued from the corners of Mr. Fu's mouth, and a smell that had permeated the divan right along grew intense in our corner — a sweet smell, suggesting incense yet distinct; heavy and with a tendency, one would suspect, to be sickening when in great volume. The smoking of the pipe took barely a minute.

"That is supposed to be Calcutta opium," Mr. Fu said when he had finished and put the pipe down. "The best opium has always come from Patna and Benares, in India, but you can't get that now unless you're lucky. The best you can get is so-called Calcutta, adulterated about five times. It is smuggled in by ship or plane. Persian opium never seems to get this far east; I have heard it is very strong. The West China opium, from Yunnan and Sikang Provinces, is not very good, but any opium except that from a few wretched small districts will give you some pleasure if it is pure. I stayed in Sikang during the war, and about one man in ten was a smoker there. You hear a good deal about opium from Dairen, in Manchuria, but the only good Dairen stuff these days is the brand called One-Three-Nine, and you never get it here any more. Dairen has really become the worst, and the cheapest. For some time now, I have heard, the Russians have been taking the morphia out of Dairen opium and selling

what is left; that is like selling whiskey without alcohol."
Mr. Fu spoke so quietly it was almost a whisper; our
alcove seemed like an after-lights party in some boarding-
school dormitory. "All opium dealers nowadays are
crooks, of course. It's no good going to the police, because it is all illegal. If you go out in the evening with
money to buy opium and are cheated, the only thing to
do is get a like amount of money and start again." I asked
him if the Chinese Communists were selling West China
opium to the outside world, as some people believe on
pretty good authority. "I don't think so," he said. "I
think that is all false, though I don't know. The Communists are very righteous about opium; none is coming out
of China now; and that is why the price is going up. It is
ten Hong Kong dollars for half a mace now, or as much
as a man would smoke in a day; it used to be two dollars."
Ten Hong Kong dollars is about a dollar and a half in
American money. "It was different with the Japanese,"
Mr. Fu went on. "The Japanese pushed opium hard.
They are queer people. They mixed it and mixed it and
mixed it, adulterating it all the while, and then they put
in a chemical to strengthen it, to make up for what they
had taken out. It had a very strange taste, but people
smoked it. The Japanese also pushed the red pills — the
heroin. That is dreadful stuff, very habit forming. It also
disintegrates the gold and silver in your teeth, if you have
any."

Ah Ling had been making another pipe, and Mr. Fu
smoked this. When he was done he spoke to Ah Ling

in Cantonese and the latter went away; Mr. Fu said he was getting some crude opium to show me. The opium when it appeared was in the shape of a large gingersnap. It was the same brown in color as the gum Mr. Fu had been smoking and had somewhat the texture of licorice, though it was less tough; you could bend it a little, and then it would break weakly. Mr. Fu said it was generally sold in this cookie form or in a ball the size of an orange. It was a mysterious substance. Even in that stage it had come a long way from the poppy fields of India or China. Opium poppies have pods, and slits are cut in these during the harvest time. A gum oozes out and is either scraped off or let fall into little trays. It is collected and repeatedly cooked, kneaded and refined of dross till it is portable, in the shape we saw it in now. In the old days of good opium in volume, it was often made into big balls, or "heads" — Mr. Fu made a shape the size of a honeydew. He said these balls developed a skin round them, supposedly from contact with the air, and were then almost impossible to tamper with. They made the market relatively stable in the old days. They were too big for ordinary retail sale, but sometimes they were bought by syndicates; four men, say, would buy a ball, cut it in quarters in each other's presence, and take these home. Sometimes the heads or balls were packed in boxes, ten to a box, and a box of course stood for a good deal of wealth. Among the very rich it was once thought swanky to gamble with boxes of opium.

Mr. Fu said he knows one Chinese man who still has

five heads of Patna opium, but on the whole that unit has gone out of the traffic. What you get now is miscellaneous small bits in cookie or orange sizes, and you don't know what is in them. Whether it is good or bad, there is still a lot of work to be done before it can be smoked. The crude opium is put into a receptacle — a brass bowl the size of half a soccer ball is thought the best — and heated, diluted with water, and ground with a pestle till it is the thickness of molasses in winter. It is spread like a film on the inside of the bowl, which is then turned upside down and exposed to a naked flame, impurities being thus burned off and only fragrant matter left. The film, solid by now, is taken out, and the process repeated again and again with more crude opium till a stage is reached that the Chinese, always lovers of figurative speech, call the "thousand layers." The thousand layers are next broken into fragments, and to them is added half as much, in volume, of ash gouged from the inside of opium pipes. I was shown some of this; it is blackish, sootlike or slaglike, brittle or crumbly, a little like the cake from a tobacco pipe. It gives a "roughness," or "resistance," of texture to the final gum, Mr. Fu said, and makes it easier to handle. Water is added bit by bit, the mixture being heated the while, and the result is filtered through cloth and coarse, pulpy paper. The use of art, rather than science, is thought appropriate at this point as at all others in the cooking of opium. Attempts to go scientific and introduce things like chemists' filtering paper are ill advised, according to Mr. Fu. "Any intelligence results in no smoke," he said. After this casual filtering, a pail or so of brownish liquid remains. This is boiled down over a hot fire; water is added and it is boiled down again; and the process can be repeated a few more times if this seems wise. What remains then is opium fit for smoking, provided the crude was any good to start with. Good opium keeps indefinitely, Mr. Fu told me, after it is brought to this stage, though it dries up in time; when old it is rated a fine cure for some stomach ailments. Poor opium is inclined to get moldy or spoil in other ways.

The smoking had been scarcely halted by these explanations. Mr. Fu had had a third pipe and Ah Ling had made a fourth, which he now handed across the bench, ceremoniously as usual. Mr. Fu pressed it back on him, asking him to smoke; Ah Ling pushed it away as if he were unworthy of the honor, and there were protestations in fast Cantonese; finally Ah Ling took the pipe, as everyone seemed to know he would in the end. He smoked in a rhythm, not the rhythm of shave-and-a-haircut-bay-rum, but something like it. It seemed a bit on the flashy side, I thought, for that subdued place, but Mr. Fu didn't seem to mind. I had been listening off and on to other smokers in the alcove across the way and also in the big room, the activities of which could be heard and seen, after a fashion, through the slits in the partition; some smoked in one long draft and some in several shorter ones, but everyone inhaled deeply and fervidly; there was

always a noise while the inhaling was going on, the same
steady hiss or roar. Ah Ling made another pipe and was
again persuaded to smoke. He stopped halfway through,
though, with an expression of annoyance, and thrust a
spindle down through the opium pill into the bowl, working it around there awhile. He tried smoking again, but
the pipe didn't seem to draw well, and he called a servant
who took it away and came back with another. "The pipe
was stinking and getting clogged up," Mr. Fu said.
"Sometimes when that happens you can clear it out with
the needle, but often you must take it apart and really
clean it." When Ah Ling had smoked once more Mr. Fu
showed me the pipe. The bowl's neck was set into a hole
in the stem's side, about the size of a nickel, and Mr. Fu
took it from this socket with a direct pull — no twisting
or unscrewing. This bowl too was shaped like a doorknob, and it felt like a doorknob in the hand, though it
was hot from smoking. It was hollow and very thin,
really just a doorknob's shell. In color and texture it was
like terra cotta, though the top surface was mostly covered by a patina of opium brown, I suppose from the
rolling of pills.

"Bowls resolve themselves into two categories of texture," Mr. Fu said. "There is the hard kind, which relies
on thinness. It is thin as can be. You can tap it and break
it. It is a sounding board, a thing of tremble and trill.
The opposite texture is soft, thick, or durable, and muted.
Its virtue is that you can throw it out of a window, pick
it up and smoke it again — if you can call that a virtue.

It will last a lifetime. You can leave it to your grandsons, if you want them to be smokers. There is quite a bit of lore about bowls. There was a mother who brought her sons up on money she earned by making them. Her husband smoked, of course. Her name was Hsiang Niang, or Fragrant Lady. A man would get accustomed to one of her bowls, and then he would touch nothing else. They were looked on as pieces of art, and were sold as pieces of art. They *were* pieces of art." I asked Mr. Fu what had made them so. "It is as though you asked me to explain a great painting," he said thoughtfully. "It can't be done. The shape of the bowls was very simple, and sometimes they had gold leaf on them, and sometimes a green like that of bamboo leaves. Chinese scholars would often get attached to them and would say, 'I can't sleep without Fragrant Lady.' Of course this was looked on as an insult by her sons, a few of whom grew up to be rich. They went round to all the clubs buying up the bowls and breaking them, so they are very rare now. Before the war one would cost as much as two hundred Hong Kong dollars. Then there were the bowls with tones. I knew a Mr. Luk who had five of them in a matched set, in the five different tones. That was another thing. This noise that we make now, with this pipe, can hardly be called music. But it was music with the old pipes and the old prewar opium. There were five tones, just as you might say that do, re, mi, fa and so are five tones. They were called *fu*, which means happiness; *lu*, high government position; *shou*, longevity; *k'ang*, health; and *ning*,

orderliness. It was an achievement to have five mature
bowls in the different tones, because it takes years to
make one mature. As for the stem, you must smoke it till
it is full of thick solidified gum. And that is quite magi-
cal; one smoke with an old pipe can get you quite lifted
up. There is gum inside the bowl also, but without much
virtue because it keeps burning and passing away; it is
temporary." I took up the stem and looked in the hole
where the bowl had rested. Inside was a shiny dark-
brown mucky substance, like the mud you might expect
in a mine. It had the sweet opium smell. The stem itself
was of plain dark bamboo, and it had an ivory mouthpiece. I ran my finger down the side, and the bamboo felt
satiny. "The stems are important too," Mr. Fu said. "The
best are made of bamboo from a place called Ngaichau
Island; it has a mysterious grain that you can feel but not
see. It is also good if a bamboo pipe has a knot sticking
out from one of its joints, shaped like a knot of women's
hair, made from the stumps of twigs that were growing
there; the very best is to have the stumps of seven twigs,
properly carved. There is also a beautiful crooked wood,
called mountain mandarin, that is supposed to have medicinal qualities, and pipestems from it are valued highly.
Ordinary wood is bad, though. Ivory is good for the
mouthpiece, and especially blood ivory, which takes on
color with smoking." What was the matter with plain
wood, I asked. "Wood so near the face suggests a coffin,
for one thing. Also the Chinese character for wood and
the character for mouth combine to make the character

for idiot. Nobody," said Mr. Fu with Chinese finality, "wants to be an idiot."

Through the slits in the partition I could get a look at the big room, and from time to time I studied it. Its key qualities, I should say, were brownness, horizontality and calm. The walls and benches were brown, and so were the pipes and the faces of the smokers, which stood out in the glow of the little lamps. The murky air seemed to make things browner, and so did the opium smell, which I had come to identify with brownness entirely. The benches, which were about three feet off the ground, seemed very flat all the way round, as did the smokers on them; these to a man were in some kind of reclining pose, sometimes leaning on an elbow, more often down with head on pillow, the highest part of the body a shoulder or bent knee. They were dressed in the plain cotton clothes, usually faded and patched, of rickshaw coolies and laborers; the place was a low-class dive except for such opulence as might be lent it by visitors to the alcoves. I could get a fair idea of what the smokers were up to after Mr. Fu's and Ah Ling's explanations. Some were making pipes, others were smoking them; but at any one time most were just lying on their pillows, taking it easy. When they moved they moved slowly, and their talk was low. The Cantonese dialect normally has frequent loud spots in it, and some outsiders find it quarrelsome-sounding, but there was none of this to be heard in the divan. The mood was quiet and harmonious, like that in a cave of anemones waving their arms without passion. Opium addicts are supposed to grow thin, because they lose their appetites, and sallow; it seemed to me that many of the smokers in the room showed these qualities — an impression I confirmed later, on the way out. I could also confirm that the pupils of a smoker's eyes narrow to pinpoints when he is under the influence. This may be in line with a contraction Mr. Fu says occurs in all the body's "passages and cavities"; opium, he says, greatly hampers certain of the main body functions. It also makes people thirsty, and I noticed that each group of smokers in the divan had a pot of tea, with cups they drank down often and refilled. Servants padded through the room in their cloth shoes, tending the tea and opium supply lines. A couple of them sat at a table filling the little horn containers; a rack of pipes, hung horizontally above each other like riding crops, was attached to the wall over their heads; the pipes were simple, like the one we were using; there was no magical-grained bamboo or medicinal wood in this place. The squat man, who smiled a good deal and seemed jovial, stood by the table and moved round but little; he was plainly in charge, though I gathered from Mr. Fu and Ah Ling that some vague person of greater influence actually owned the divan or controlled it. There were a couple of lazy cats there too, a tortoiseshell and a striped yellow one, which now lay on the floor, now drifted about, quietly and in tune with the general pace. Perhaps they suppressed the rats, though they didn't suppress the cockroaches wholly; at one point a big one came out and scurried across our bench; the roaches in these latitudes are huge and active.

Mr. Fu saw me looking through the slits, and he observed that the divan was typical of the poorer-class ones; it was not a place a scholar of old would have picked for his smoking. "There are four things that are supposed to make smoking good," he said, "and in my opinion they are solid facts — not just talking, like so much a Chinese literary man says when he starts making sets of good things, in fours or other numbers. One good thing is the noise of soft rain on the windowpane; I don't think this is just an aesthetic point; I think it is a key to the amount of humidity that's best for smoking. Another good thing is a lamp that is clear, or brilliant — however you translate the character *ming*, the one made up from the characters for sun and moon. A third is the big noise of the pipe; without the noise there is no smoke; you wouldn't feel you were smoking; indeed you wouldn't *be* smoking. Finally, and much the most important, is friendship; think of De Quincey and the mess he got into from taking opium alone; it is not so much fun alone; that's why it's so dangerous. Anyway, a man of the leisure class would try hard to get those four things; and when he had them he would expect very enjoyable smoking. Those refinements are beyond the reach of these poor people here."

It seemed to get pleasanter all the time in our alcove, even though we didn't have quite all the four good things.

It was snug; it was warm, and it looked warmer because of the lamp's orange light. Mr. Fu and Ah Ling had each had several pipes, and they seemed talkative. I judged it was time to ask Mr. Fu, who was lying dreamily with his legs crossed, what effect opium had on a smoker. "Well, it jolts you right out of the blues," he said. "When you are in the dumps, it will make you feel everyone is reaching out towards you with sympathy. Your whole desire is to *do* things, together with a friend or friends, not separately. Smoking makes you gregarious. You start talking; you never grow silent. You want to *do* things because you can do everything better than other people can. If you gamble, you gamble to lose, because you can lose better than others, lose with less hurt; it doesn't help a damn bit to win. Alcohol makes a swine out of a gentleman, some people say, but opium makes a gentleman out of a swine." He was talking deliberately and seemed to be taking much thought. "Very good opium is slow in its effect. It takes three quarters of an hour to feel it. Of course you can't compare now with the old days because of the terrible gulf of the war. Prewar you could get really good Calcutta. You could feel it going down, though you can't now. You could feel an actual warmth going downwards, but now it's not so palpable. I think the most terrific thing is the physical aspect. A man in a crawling mood would speed up very much from opium. He might lick you badly in a tennis game if he had been your equal before. He could make the ball go like a bullet. I don't know if a hundred-yard runner would improve his record, but a tennis player would be better. Once when I was younger I was playing in a championship tennis tournament in a Far Eastern city. I was winning a match easily, and then the opium gave out on me; I lost every point after that; I am absent-minded, and I didn't realize till some time later what had slowed me down. That is another thing about opium — its secretiveness. It is like the works of God; not seen, not heard; it is felt without your knowing. Time is just suspended. The nearest I can get to describing it is in terms of gears, big wheels and small ones; the mind and the body are in different gears. You might lie here for days, and people would see you all the time. But you would think at the end you had been here for only a few hours."

The lamp's flame was burning low, and Ah Ling took the chimney off, nudged the wick aside and filled the reservoir from the little teapot. "Smoking steadies me up for writing," Mr. Fu murmured. "It is like a wonderful surgical instrument — dangerous if you don't limit it. It will help your thoughts to fly over the cosmos. You will get exactly nowhere, though, unless you have your goal all planned out, fixed in advance of the opium. It will make you lose the sense of time passing, and unless you take care in advance you will plunge in the wrong direction, to things that are not concrete. You could communicate with Bernard Shaw, but not with everyone. The wonder of opium is there for you to use, and it makes you fly through all that space. You sit here all concrete and factual, yet really you are flying." He raised himself on an elbow. "Here is a solid fact," he said. "Every writer knows the moment when words will not come with ease. Opium then just plucks them out of the back of your cranium, with a surprise to you each time. Then sometimes the words tumble over each other, if you are going well. I should underline, though, that this happens only with good opium, not with bad."

I asked him about De Quincey, who got his effects by drinking laudanum, a tincture of opium. "Everything De Quincey said was true," he answered, "with the natural and inevitable exaggeration. But of course eating or drinking opium is bad; it can only be a pale imitation. It should be kept as a fall-back for breaking off the habit of smoking; it is the natural and most successful way of doing that. One trouble with De Quincey must have been that he lost count of the drops — you remember that he writes of having taken so many thousand drops a day. Inevitably he would leave off dropping it from a medicine dropper and start pouring it. Then he would lose control." After De Quincey became an addict, I remembered, he was troubled by vivid and horribly present nightmares, which seem to have lingered with him through the suspension of time described by Mr. Fu. I asked if addiction to smoking brought the same thing. "No," Mr. Fu said. "The trouble with De Quincey wasn't the DTs or pink elephants or anything like that from opium. It is possible that the laudanum, in all that quantity, gave him indigestion. Anyway, smoking doesn't give you dreams like that. The danger of smoking is that when you lose control there is no compensation except to increase. Then you are gone, though some addicts, mind you, have kept on for forty years and recovered. An addict can still get a lift from opium; his trouble is that he can't do without it. It is true he may get thin and weak, but I believe this often comes from a general loss of healthiness, or even from age, rather than from opium alone. We Chinese call opium smoking taming the tiger, and anyone knows you don't enter a tiger's cage without risk. Even so, half the habit is psychological. I have known addicts who have been fooled into smoking mud for a month and haven't known it — pure mud, no opium at all; a cat could have eaten it all and not died."

I don't know how to rate these judgments of Mr. Fu's beyond saying they are on the rosy side of a broad spectrum of opinions about opium. Some experts I have talked with believe the road into addiction is easy, the road out very hard, and the usefulness of an addict almost zero. But many other experts would agree with Mr. Fu.

The smoking was over, apparently, and we lay there awhile, talking in a desultory way. Mr. Fu told me of a songbird he had once owned, which he had let fly about his room at will; the bird had got interested in opium and had tried to eat some, but had managed only to get its bill stuck together; after that it had given up trying direct indulgence, but had continued to like the general idea of opium sessions; it had come to Mr. Fu eagerly whenever he got his pipe out, had perched on his hand, arm or shoulder, and had refused to leave till the smoking was over; it had kept this up for more than a year, till it finally disappeared one day though an open window in a typhoon.

At length we decided we had had enough repose, and Mr. Fu bade Ah Ling send for the manager, who came smiling. We had some conversation with him, during which I learned indirectly, through Mr. Fu's interpreting, that business in the divan was about as good as usual; that roughly the same people came night after night, with a few exceptions like ourselves, and smoked roughly the same amount; that they were expected to keep coming as long as they were given good stuff at a reasonable price; and that this was getting harder all the time, but was still possible. The manager fidgeted; though affable, he plainly didn't want to talk, and I stopped quizzing him. Mr. Fu paid him, and we got up.

We were delayed at the door while the manager sent down to make sure the street was empty. The smoker on the bench nearest us was a tall man and very thin; his face was pale and drawn, and he looked a good deal like the Mad Hatter except that he was wearing a knitted skull-cap of brown wool; he was languidly stroking the tortoise-shell cat, which had somehow gotten to that place on its rounds; he seemed dirty and his clothes were carelessly buttoned, yet there was an air of courtesy to him; he graciously beckoned me to sit down and join him in a pipe, something I truly regretted I couldn't do. Just then the scout came back to say the coast was clear, and we started down the stairs. Once we were outside, Ah Ling

vanished; he didn't go away, it seemed; he just disinte-
grated. The air was sharply cool now, and I remarked on
this to Mr. Fu. "Yes," he said, "but after the opium, you
know, I feel that a cold night is just what is wanted.
That wind coming down the alley is just right too. It has
all been laid out in perfect harmony. That's how it always is when you've been smoking."

The New City

A NEW CITY is a rare thing, and the new city of Chandigarh, in India, is being planned by a rare man, the French
architect Le Corbusier. It is an event of global, if not cos-
mic, import, and it may cause talk for centuries. Chandigarh is designed as a capital for the East Punjab, a new
Indian province whose birth pangs have been great.
The entire Punjab — East and West together — is a vast,
rich plain, nearly five hundred miles long, stretched out
in northwest India below the Himalayas. At independence it was split in two, according to the prevailing faith
of the inhabitants — the Muslim West going to Pakistan
and the Hindu East to India. This entailed big migrations
— for Hindus and Muslims permeated each other's halves
— and they were made not gently but violently, with
massacres that shocked the world then, in 1947. Nearly
everyone in the Punjab was affected, and rehabilitation
has been in order ever since. In the East Punjab a new

capital has been in order too, to replace Lahore, the Punjab's old seat of learning and government, which fell to Pakistan. Chandigarh is the answer, and a controversial one. Corbusier attracts controversy, for one thing. New cities do too. So do Western attempts to organize Eastern life now. Hence there are arguments about Chandigarh in places like New Delhi, the Indian capital. Some think it ill starred — that the East Punjab will fail as a unit, and Chandigarh with it. Some think it an imposition — "a city designed by Europeans for unfortunate Hindus," as an Indian friend of mine called it recently. Many others, of course, think Chandigarh an upward step for India and civilization. People in India chat back and forth along these lines, and the press does too. I had been hearing them since I reached New Delhi a few months ago, and recently I went up to Chandigarh and had a look.

The trip was over a hundred miles, straight north, and it took half a day on the train, with a bad connection at a nearby Punjab town called Ambala. This is one thing Chandigarh's critics complain of — they say the capital should have been tacked on to Ambala or some other town with existing communications, instead of being placed, as it has been, in comparative wilderness. I could see what they meant, but the point didn't trouble me much, as the scenery was all new and pleasant — not wearying. The North Indian climate is deadly hot in summer, but in the cool months it is delightful beyond words, with crystal air and chill mornings that thaw toward noon, as the sun glows in the blue sky. Now, in early winter, this warm sunlight fell on old tan grass or on brown earth through which the green sprouts of new wheat were coming up. Birds were everywhere when I looked out the window. I shared my compartment with two Sikhs, members of a special sect — an offshoot of Hinduism — that is centered in the Punjab. Sikh men wear beards and turbans; they are big and strapping as a rule, and are common in the Indian Army. One of my companions now was an army officer, and his turban was black, whereas that of the other, a civilian, was pink. We talked, read and looked out the window, and in due course arrived at the new Chandigarh station, on a spur. I made my way to the hotel — a ten-minute drive — established myself there, rented a bicycle, applied to see Corbusier, and began exploring the place.

Chandigarh is on a plain that tilts slightly — on a one per cent grade — away from the foothills of the Himalayas. These hills dominate the site along the northeastern edge. They are dark green, and in winter they usually have some puffy clouds above them, amid the azure. They are always in the background as you look across the site from the downhill side, the foreground being covered with tawny grass broken here and there by new buildings. At first glance these buildings seem scattered almost at random, but actually they are set in a gridiron scheme that divides the site — fifteen square miles in all — into some twenty-five sectors. The sectors will be largely self-sufficient, according to the plan, with their own schools and shopping centers, and fast traffic will be kept out of them.

I soon learned that Chandigarh's main points of interest, so far, are a couple of nearly completed residential sectors, at the town's lower edge, and the "capitol complex," a plot at its upper edge, against the mountains, where the main public buildings will be. These points are more than two miles apart. The Mountview Hotel, where I stayed, is in the fields between them. The architects' office is some distance to one side of this axis, and the temporary secretariat, where a skeleton crew is running the Punjab Government, is off to another side. Under the circumstances — and as few Indians own cars — bicycles are a common sight in Chandigarh. After five, when the offices close, little flocks of homing bicycles can be met on certain roads, bearing Sikh clerks with turbans and non-Sikh ones without. The flocks will presumably grow bigger along with the city.

The capitol complex, I learned, will be the showy part of Chandigarh, with four buildings — the Governor's House, Assembly, High Court and Secretariat — all designed by Corbusier himself. One of them, the High Court, was nearly finished when I was there, and after my first day Corbusier sent word that he would show me this. I repaired there to meet him at nine in the morning and found an unprecedented structure, equipped among other things with a "parasol," or extra roof to keep the hot sun off the proper one. It was rectangular — seventy feet high by three hundred and fifty-four feet long, I

learned later — and when I approached it from the front
— one of the broad sides — what I saw was a big concrete
frame, like a box but on the scale of an airplane hangar
or block of grain elevators. The long top side of this was
the parasol, and beneath it, standing almost free, was the
true building itself, housing the courtrooms and offices.
The front of this was honeycombed with "sun-breakers"
of reinforced concrete — open-ended boxes designed to
keep out the high summer sun and let in the low sun of
winter. It looked like a magnified wall of pigeonholes in
a post office, but less monotonous, for the boxes were
varied somewhat in size or shape. From behind them
came the glitter of window glass. Workmen were in the
pigeonholes, finishing the windows, and they were squatting or sitting — they didn't quite have room to stand.
This honeycombed building was about fifty feet high,
and it stood under the flat parasol, which, however, came
down to meet it periodically in a series of uprights between parabolic arches — giving an effect somewhat like
the underside of the she-wolf that nursed Romulus and
Remus. In the arches — the spaces between the nursing
apparatus, so to speak — there was great room for breezes
to blow through, over the true roof, on which the sun
would never fall.

I stood there awaiting Corbusier and taking in the
scene. The building was nearly finished, but not quite,
and numbers of men and women were working round
it — Indian laborers, still barely touched by the machine
age. Women were carrying basins, or shallow baskets,

of earth on their heads — these were put up there by male helpers, and the heads themselves were protected by washerlike cloth pads. Piles of dirt, red and brown, lay about. The women walked along with great suppleness, one after the other, wearing cotton shawls in red and yellow — the Punjabi peasants like a strong yellow that leans toward orange, like scrambled eggs with catsup in them, and there were many touches of this. The women wore thick silver anklets as well, and their bare feet were brown. Now and then a flock of white donkeys came by, also bearing dirt. Three turbaned Sikh watchmen, or straw bosses, surveyed the scene, and there was a constant background noise of tamping, pounding, hammering and chopping with primitive tools. These age-old sights and sounds enveloped the improbable, futuristic building before me.

Corbusier was driven up in a jeep, got out, and looked rather futuristic himself. He wore a khaki suit, a black-and-white checked shirt, a blue-and-red bow tie, and spectacles with very thick dark shell rims. He had a dark-brown felt hat. His face was ruddy and his hair nearly white. His eyes were blue-gray, and later I noted that they had a faraway look when he was explaining things. His expression was dead-pan. He greeted me and started at once for the building, I following in his wake.

He took me through the main entrance — a vast space, really open air, going clear up to the parasol — and then round to the back. Sun-breakers of another kind were installed there — big horizontal slabs of concrete, fixed be-

tween pillars that stood back from the building like buttresses. The winter sun was slanting in over them now,
and striking the walls and windows. "Sun-breakers work
like the opening of a camera," Corbusier said, "closing
the sun off in summer, letting him in winter. In summer
this will all be shade." I could see what he meant. At a
high angle no sun would get past the slabs at all. They
were like an open Venetian blind. "Sun-breakers are my
invention," Corbusier went on, slowly, painstakingly —
he spoke English for my sake, and it wasn't easy for him.
"They are scientifically calculated," he said. "They al-
low for the latitude, and the orientation of the building.
For the position of the sun through the year." He spoke
slowly because of the English, but it seemed to suit him
anyway. He seemed deliberate in his manner, and concentrated.

He put his hand on the concrete, which was rough and
gray — unfinished — and he said it would be left that
way. "For fifty years concrete has been treated as a poor
material," he said, "but here it is treated as noble. It is
left — what do you say? — rough. It is like stone of the
mountains. It has its own harmony." The gray concrete
was streaked with brown — I suppose from the dirt that
had gone into it — and there were swirls of gravel here
and these, and bubble holes in the surface. Corbusier
pointed to these and to the marks left by the joints in the
wooden forms. He said it would all remain unchanged.
This gray of new concrete was everywhere, in the walls

and floor and the buttresslike pillars; it would set the tone for the building's whole outside, I gathered.

Corbusier led me through a back door into one of the courtrooms — a high, rectangular chamber, looking out frontwards through the windows and big gray pigeon-holes — and there, on the wall behind the judge's bench, he showed me a tapestry he had designed himself. It was about twenty-five feet square and mainly abstract, done in wool, with rectangles of blue, beige, black, gray and near-white. Its only representational figures were the outlines of one hand and two feet, spotted unobtrusively in certain rectangles, and I have since been told that this tapestry, and others Corbusier is doing for the High Court, are far more abstract than the paintings for which he is known. "Tapestries will be in every courtroom because of acoustical necessity," he told me now, and added that he was designing them all. They were being woven at Amritsar, a nearby city, in an Indian technique used mainly for rough cotton fabrics, but adaptable for wool too.

Corbusier said that the acoustics of these rooms were very good — he indulged in no false modesty during our session — and when he mentioned this I realized that I no longer heard the background hammering and thumping that surrounded the building. The sides of this room were done in acoustical material that looked like white plaster, and the front, of course, was mainly of glass, with the honeycomb of sun-breakers beyond it. A workman was sitting up in a sun-breaker now — puttying a window, so far as I could tell.

We left the courtroom — emerging into the realm of hammering once more — and went back to the spacious main entrance. This was paved with near-white flagstones, set in rows of different widths. "They are different sizes because they come that way from the quarry," Corbusier said, fumbling before the word "quarry" came out. "We can use all sizes, and that is cheaper," he added, and explained that he harmonized the different sizes by what he calls his Modulor principle. From what he told me then, and from later reading, I understand that this is a scale of measurements worked out by Corbusier some years ago, based on the Golden Mean of the Greeks and the Renaissance, but keyed to the human figure. He said it was derived from mathematics and would assure good proportions when rightly used in a building, and he compared it with human-scale measuring systems of the Egyptians and Japanese. "The Modulor makes peace between foot-inch and decimal numbers." He spoke disparagingly of feet and inches, which the British had bequeathed to India.

"Anglo-Saxons do not know what difficulty is caused by the foot-inch," he said, "which does not obey to the decimal system." He spoke slowly and thoughtfully, in a low voice and thoroughly French accent. His gray eyes got their faraway look when he came to something especially important or hard to translate. His face was dead-pan all the time. He seemed a very serious man, as if thoughtfully staking everything on his theories — almost in the way Napoleon must have staked everything on his battles, it occurred to me. He had the air of knowing his game and playing it coolly.

From behind this open entrance a ramp led upward, zigzagging back and forth like stairs, but more gradual in slope, to a higher story of offices above the courtrooms. We started climbing this. Women passed us with loads on their heads. "Here the machine is not used for carrying," Corbusier said. "Here the problem is to employ as many people as possible. People are very cheap, but they must eat." And as he spoke, quietly, he turned his faraway gaze toward me. He was theorizing some more, I mused — summarizing Asia — and being much to the point too, I thought. And he turned and continued upward. He walked briskly and stiffly — erect — with his elbows a little bit out.

Outside the upper offices were more sun-breakers, and Corbusier pointed to these. "Sun-breakers are a Corbusier invention," he said gravely, "and that is one reason why certain people don't use them." He explained about the ventilation up there too, which would pass through holes in the interior walls, as well as through the windows, so the breeze would flow constantly through the building in warm weather, from front to back or vice versa. The whole city was based on wind orientation, he said, with ventilators to take advantage of it.

For the most part, the windows of the High Court building were made from big fixed pieces of glass, but in between these were narrow vertical spaces, each closed by a wooden shutter on hinges. Corbusier said the shutters were his invention, worked out on the Côte d'Azur. He showed me fly screens too, and told me every opening in the building would have them; and he said this was another thing he had worked out in the Côte d'Azur, thereby creating a mosquito-free house. He seemed as proud of this achievement as the others, though I felt it was behind the times — in parts of Asia they have begun spraying whole cities with DDT, and as I remember it the fully screened building was common in America in the thirties. But I didn't question him. I had faith in his originality, and I assumed this was just a small instance where the continents were out of step.

We went up onto the roof — not the parasol, but the true roof beneath it — and from there we got a fine view of the surroundings. The site of the main town sloped down from us to one side, with its scattered buildings far away in the fields. On the other side rose the green mountains, with the blue sky and clouds above them. "The site is marvelous," Corbusier said. "It is a big chance, to have such a view. The men who chose it, Thapar and Verma" — he named two Indian officials — "are big men." He gestured toward the mountains. "The landscape all over is free," he said, and he explained that there would be no further building along this upper edge besides the capitol complex itself — and the complex would be screened from the city below by trees, and by small hills made with dirt removed from foundations, ponds and sunken roads. All the motor roads in the capitol complex would be sunken, Corbusier said, and a viewer on the ground would see no cars.

He showed me where the other buildings would be, close by in the foreground. The Secretariat's foundation was begun, but the Governor's House and Assembly were marked only by timbers laid on the ground. Near them was the model of a mobile that would stand there — a giant human hand with upraised palm. From sketches I saw later I should say that the whole group will be spectacular, to put it mildly. The Governor's House is to have a big trough-shaped parasol with a roof garden in it, where concerts can be held. The Secretariat is to be nine stories high, on concrete stilts, and will be served by ramps on which the hundreds of clerks may stream up and down at rush hours. It will have an egg-shaped concrete water tank on the roof. To judge by these sketches, and by the example of the High Court, all the capitol buildings will be imaginative, singular and open to controversy — and a goal for pilgrims long into the future.

The High Court's parasol no longer made me think of a she-wolf as we stood beneath it. It was all of gray concrete. Its outer edges, on the long sides, overhung the building proper by about twenty feet. They were straight and true against the blue sky as we looked up at them, and from them the concrete surface curved down toward us to form the arches and their intervening supports. It was the kind of curvature — precise yet subtle —

that one sees on an airplane fuselage. Corbusier said it was a neat job of design. "From the horizontal to the *parabole*," he said. "A nice thing in static calculation."

We turned away and started down, and as we did so we passed a workman spraying gunite — a substance that hardens to look like rough stucco — on a wall. He was squatting on a brick floor. "He is supposed to put something on the bricks to protect them," Corbusier said to me, "but now they will be covered with gunite." He shrugged. "I don't protest," he said. "It's not my job. I just make the plans and they build it." We were walking down the ramp by now. "The workers here are very clever," he said. "They work with their feet even." He paused and turned to me with his concentrated, faraway look, behind the dark-rimmed glasses. "The work is very rough, but here you must take consideration of particular realities." We walked on down, and through the entrance, and out to the building's front again. We looked back there, at the great expanse of cement pigeonholes and the windows glittering behind them. "You see it is all glass," Corbusier said, "but the sun will never be dangerous. He will not be the enemy, but the friend." And then he left me. He just walked away.

P. L. Verma, one of the "big men" whom Corbusier had mentioned, was in Chandigarh during my visit, and I saw the other, P. N. Thapar, in New Delhi later. Mr. Verma, the East Punjab's chief engineer — a tall, strong-faced, middle-aged man — is in charge of the city's construction. His office is near that of the architects, and he has just moved into a new home near the High Court, these points being about a mile apart on the tilted plain. He has been on the job since it was first envisioned, in 1947. Mr. Thapar came into the picture in 1949, the project having meanwhile been delayed by doubts and political squabbles. Thapar is a member of the Indian Civil Service, an elite corps of administrators developed by the British. At independence there were a few hundred Indian — as opposed to British — I.C.S. men in the country, and some observers think they have staved off chaos during these years. Verma's role with Chandigarh has been technical, but Thapar's, during the two and a half years it lasted, was more generally administrative. He functioned as an expediter, we might say, and in this he was backed not only by the Punjab, but by the Central Indian Government and Prime Minister Nehru, who has taken a personal interest in Chandigarh.

Thapar and Verma went to Europe in the fall of 1950, looking for an architect. They visited Italy, Switzerland, France, Belgium, Holland and England. Architects in some of these countries were keen enough on the idea, but loath to work in India because of the climate — Italian and Dutch architects both dropped out for this reason. When Corbusier was interviewed in France he liked the proposition at once and was willing to take low pay for it, though not, it seems, through any vague Bohemianism. He is a hardheaded businessman, Thapar says, and he behaved like one at the time. But he settled for two thousand rupees a month plus expenses on his visits to India, which occur twice yearly and last several weeks. At such times he draws a total of some four thousand rupees monthly, or between eight and nine hundred dollars. This is his pay as planner. He also gets, as an architect's fee, three per cent of the cost of any building he designs personally. Nobody concerned thinks these payments are much. The job is thought to be mainly a labor of love for Corbusier — or a labor on behalf of his theories. He is almost seventy, it is pointed out, and thus far many of these theories are untried except on paper.

Besides Corbusier, Thapar and Verma hired three other first-rank European architects: Maxwell Fry and his wife Jane Drew, from Great Britain, and Corbusier's cousin Pierre Jeanneret from France (Corbusier's real name is Charles-Edouard Jeanneret, and "Le Corbusier," or "The Crow," is a pseudonym). In theory Corbusier's job was to complete the layout and design the capitol complex, while the others designed various buildings independently. Miss Drew has written that her and Fry's relationship with Corbusier was defined for them as follows: "He is there for you to ask his advice; you must take it or not as you think proper." Many people who see Chandigarh, or hear of it, are unaware of this autonomy. The view of other architects, one gathers, is that Fry, Jeanneret and Miss Drew have each done distinguished work at Chandigarh that will long be celebrated for itself; but to the public the place seems virtually to be a one-man Corbusier city, in whose designing the Master has chanced to have talented help. Corbusier's personality and reputation are so strong, it seems, that those of others tend to give way before them.

Living quarters for three thousand families have already gone up at Chandigarh in the two residential sectors so far developed — Sectors Twenty-two and Twenty-three, they are called. Virtually all of these have been built by the government for its employees — as yet private capital has achieved only two or three dozen houses at Chandigarh, though in the end it is supposed to account for eighty to ninety per cent of the total. These government quarters fall into thirteen classes, according to the rank, and earning power, of the tenants. Many architects in doing buildings for Asia are induced to dress them up with Asian motifs — bubbly domes in India, for instance, or swoop-eaved roofs in China. Corbusier and his associates have resisted this idea, if it was ever pressed on them. Their houses look "modern," or "functional," in the popular sense. They are one or two stories high, standing singly or in blocks. In shape they are cubical or oblong (which goes well with Indian life, for many Indians sleep on their roofs in the hot weather). They are bound together not only by their design but by their materials, the main one being brick, which is cheap at Chandigarh and is seen everywhere there apart from the capitol complex. The bricks are a rich, warm red, rather brownish, and give a substantial look. Often they are set off by trim of white-painted plaster, which adds a smart touch like that of white-walled tires or white gloves.

Sun-breakers are seen everywhere. Some are concrete boxes placed outside windows, like those on the High Court. They can be deep or shallow according to their orientation — those facing south need less depth than those facing southwest, say, as the hot-weather sun stands above the former at midday, but slants toward the latter in afternoon. A deep sun-breaker can project a couple of feet, and when you look out through it from inside you might be in a thick-walled medieval fortress.

A simpler type of sun-breaker consists merely of alternate bricks laid crosswise, so their ends jut out like studs to shade a bit of the wall below them. This trick is used often at Chandigarh and gives a pleasant rough texture to the brickwork. Anything that juts out and casts a shadow, really, is a sun-breaker — even a single narrow ledge — and so there are many projections giving depth to Chandigarh's walls. When the sun hits them slantwise it throws diagonal shadows on these walls, reinforcing the geometrical look of the buildings, and the whole thing fits together well. Brick or concrete lattices are common too — openwork walls on verandas or around roofs. They are called *jalli* work, from an old Indian word — used most often, in the past, for wrought-metal screens. They act as sun-breakers — casting shade while letting in breeze — and they give privacy of a sort. They too give rough wall textures. I have read that Corbusier's architecture, over the years, has emphasized rough textures and cubical forms. This is certainly true of Chandigarh, though these residential quarters were designed not by him, but by his associates.

Each residential sector at Chandigarh is a rectangle half a mile by three quarters of a mile, tilting upward, in the long direction, toward the mountains. The sectors are like the neighborhoods of our American cities in that they have their own schools and shopping centers. Housewives and children can stay in them for days on end, presumably. Fast traffic is kept outside them — kept to the grid that separates them one from another. The classification of traffic is one of Corbusier's main ideas at Chandigarh, in fact, and he has divided the roads there into seven types. The first three of these — called V1, V2 and V3 — are all for high-speed traffic, and the gridiron is made up chiefly of the V3 class, which carries city-wide transport. Each sector is bounded by four of these V3 roads, as a rule. Then it is bisected, on the short axis, by a V4 road, or shopping street, which in turn is crossed, if only on paper as yet, by a broad green strip running up the long axis. The parks, playgrounds and schools will be on these green strips, which will look toward the mountains and thus get a maximum of nature into their total effect. The remaining slower classes of road are all internal to the sectors: V5 roads are winding affairs that circulate within them, bearing local traffic; V6 are driveways, more or less; and V7 are paths, for bicycles and pedestrians.

*   *   *

As might be expected, the more staid Punjabis can't take all of Corbusier in stride. The judges of the High Court almost rebelled against his tapestries recently, when they learned what they would be like. "For God's sake burn them or do something," one of them implored Mr. Thapar. Others scornfully likened the whole structure to a pigeon house. For a while it seemed as if the tapestries would not survive, but Corbusier won the day — according to a colleague of his at Chandigarh — by going to the "highest authority," which one assumes was Nehru. Since then he has said the High Court people showed much tolerance in accepting the tapestries, and indeed tolerance seems to be the general Punjabi, and Indian, approach to him. India understands idea-men and treats them well — perhaps better than any other country — and Corbusier benefits from this. One Punjabi at Chandigarh remarked to me, with amusement, that Corbusier had had many big jobs before, but had somehow always parted company with them rather early — that Chandigarh was the first place where he had been kept on for a matter of years. "Of course he's mad about India as a result," the Punjabi added, laughing.

This tolerance at Chandigarh is mixed with some resigned criticism and not a little discomfort. The worst complaint seems to be that few verandas have been built in the city because of the emphasis on sun-breakers. Verandas are sun-breakers themselves, of course, but of a type less new, and hence perhaps less fascinating, than

those Chandigarh really goes in for. Verandas have long
been popular in India and other hot parts of Asia, as
places that can be shady in summer, sunny in winter, and
fairly rainproof all the time — so you can leave furniture and other things out on them. Indians often treat
their verandas as extra rooms, and spend much time
there. In Chandigarh the verandas have been omitted
from most government housing on the grounds that they
are expensive, and that to build real rooms, protected by
sun-breakers, is a better use of the space. Chandigarh
veranda lovers, however, feel that their tastes have been
ignored through foreign caprice.

Some tenants at Chandigarh dislike the *jallis* — the
brick or concrete lattices — because dust blows in
through them. Some of the older women dislike the
Western-type stoves in the kitchens, because by custom
Punjabis sit on the floor to cook. They complain too that
there is no room for *tandoors*, special jarlike ovens for
baking *chapatis* — wheat pancakes — a Punjab staple. And
many Punjabi families like to keep a buffalo — keeping
it almost in the household and feeding it on scraps — and
this is ruled out entirely in the plan. The architects' inexperience with India is blamed for these things, and
also for the small size of the houses, which one is repeatedly told have been designed with modern Western
families in mind — two parents and a few children —
whereas Indian families often include grandparents,
aunts, uncles and cousins. These many-membered Indian

households usually keep a number of *charpoys*, or string beds, on hand, which at night are set out to turn the rooms — or the roof in summer — into a sea of sleeping area, but which by day must be upended and stored somewhere. Chandigarh's tenants say there isn't enough room for this, and again they blame the foreignness of the architects.

The latter reply that inflated costs are what keep the houses small: that the higher Punjab officials, the ones who complain on this score, can't hope for the spaciousness they are used to — in government houses built, say, in the thirties — unless their housing at Chandigarh is subsidized like that of the peons. As for the high stoves, the architects say the new generation of Punjabi women will be getting used to chairs anyway, and to standing up. Buffaloes, they say, cannot possibly be attached to households in a modern city. The point about *tandoor* ovens they seem to concede, for they are trying to make room for them in plans of government houses not yet built. The objections to *jalli* work do not impress them. And so it goes.

Whatever their worries, the Chandigarh citizens have plenty to talk about. There aren't many places, after all, where you can loose a flood of conversation by merely saying "*jalli*" or "sun-breaker." Or, better still, by saying "Corbusier." Corbusier is a great figure in Chandigarh, even though he visits it but twice a year and keeps rather to himself then. Everyone seems in awe of him. When I presented myself to the public-relations staff of the Punjab Government, for instance, they offered at once to show me everything except Corbusier himself. "M. Le Corbusier does things in his own way," they said in hushed tones — they advised me how to make an approach, but did not make it for me.

Corbusier might be more intimate with the neighbors if it weren't for the language problem. As it is, he and Jeanneret see a good deal of the higher officials, but to communicate with them they have much recourse to gestures and sketching. Corbusier lives with Jeanneret when at Chandigarh — while I was there they were moving to one of the higher-class new official residences, designed by Jeanneret himself, near the High Court. Jeanneret is said by experts to be a gifted architect, but he seems destined to spend his life in his older cousin's shadow — a fate he apparently accepts gladly, it should be added. The pair live very simply at Chandigarh, by all accounts, with a minimum of servants, for India, and with primitive furniture that Jeanneret has contrived from things like bricks and tree trunks. Corbusier is said to have a French liking for wines and a dislike for milk, which he can't bear even in puddings. He and Jeanneret spend a good deal of time visiting the nearby villages and studying the peasant arts and crafts there — they believe, it is said, that primitive people always make things that are artistically good till they are corrupted by the lure of "calendar art." So the villages attract them. Corbusier makes sketches of what they find there, and Jeanneret takes photographs — he is credited with a fine collection of these. One gathers that Corbusier and Jeanneret have a sympathetic feeling for India, and vice versa.

Verma and Thapar are both great admirers of Corbusier, and Thapar says the two and a half years he spent with him were the best of his life. "He is a man of very strong will," Thapar told me in New Delhi. "A very bold man. He loves a controversy. But he is a truly great architect." Thapar had been much impressed because Corbusier had built the High Court straight from the drawing board — without making a model in three dimensions — and then had not changed it while the building was in progress. "This man's architecture is based on mathematics," Thapar said, "and beautified by mathematics. So he can't change the details without changing the whole thing. Nowhere would he deviate for someone else's idea of beauty." Thapar is middle-aged and sophisticated, yet he spoke of Corbusier with the enthusiasm of a small boy. "He is a good businessman," Thapar said, "but he wouldn't think of putting up a building if he didn't want to. He has turned down bank sites in India, for instance. He just wasn't interested in them." Thapar called Corbusier a philosopher and a sociologist — avocations well thought of in India — and said he had a good appreciation of Pandit Nehru's outlook on life. Corbusier and Nehru had had long conversations in Thapar's presence, he said, though he hadn't understood these because they were in French.

Thapar said Corbusier could be induced to change a plan, but had to do it in his own way. If a change was insisted on he would withdraw mutely, and then would reappear the next day with a new plan meeting the objection, but strictly in Corbusier style. At first, according to Thapar, he had wanted to make the Chandigarh Secretariat a skyscraper — verticality in modern cities being a Corbusier principle — but he had dropped the idea when told that elevators couldn't be maintained reliably there. Even so, Chandigarh, though horizontal, had the Corbusier stamp on it, as anyone could see. Thapar talked on some about Corbusier, fondly, and then concluded. "He is a domineering person," he said. "Discussion with him is a furious affair. But it's a pleasure to work with him. You're conscious all the time you're working with an architect, an artist."

While visiting Chandigarh I got the impression that Corbusier was rather solitary. It occurred to me that an artist's job is to harmonize scattered elements in some original way, and that while doing so he must guard his ideas from premature veto by others. This must be especially hard for an architect, I began to see, because his product concerns the client so intimately. And it must be harder still if the architect is dealing with new, questionable ideas, on a strange continent, and doing it on the scale of a whole city. The more I thought about this, the more I wondered whether a temperament other than Corbusier's could have put Chandigarh over.

*　　*　　*

I stayed in Chandigarh for most of a week, living in the Mountview. My room, and every room, had a big expanse of glass — windows and folding doors — on the side toward the mountains, and the sunrise was glorious there, coming up in brilliant yellows, reds and greens over the dark skyline. In the daytime I bicycled around on the V3 roads — straight bands of asphalt, they were, in the brown grass. Usually I had them to myself, except for meeting the odd truck or gang of coolies. Once I collided with a white donkey, a member of a flock carrying dirt. We approached head on and were indecisive about which way to pass. So I ran into him. One of my handlebars got caught in the girth of his paniers, and he galloped off in confusion, dragging the bicycle and leaving me seated in the road. But we got straight in the end. That was near the High Court, where I used to go and watch people at work. From there it would take me ten or fifteen minutes — down a grade scarcely noticeable for bicycling — to reach Sector Twenty-Two, where I would watch people at leisure. Chandigarh was a fine place, it turned out, for studying urban matters amid clear rustic air, but I suppose all that may change in a decade.

Before leaving I saw Corbusier once more, in his office. He was seated at a big flat drawing table and was dressed as before, except that he had his coat off. The sleeves of his blue checked shirt were rolled up, and his hands and forearms looked strong. His face was expressionless behind the dark-rimmed glasses. I asked about the general plan of Chandigarh, and he told me he had devised the "7V" formula some years earlier, while working out a master plan for Bogotá. "Bogotá is laid out on the Spanish square, the *cuadra*," he said, which is three hundred feet on a side. It was made for the horse and the ox. It is too small for modern traffic, so a larger unit is needed. The sectors at Chandigarh are six Spanish squares wide by eleven long. That was the birth of the 7V theory."

He took paper and a lead pencil and crosshatched an area into squares. Then he drew an oblong on top of this — six squares by eleven — in red crayon. "One sector," he wrote beside it, returning to the lead pencil, "contains five thousand to twenty-five thousand people — equals an urban unity for habitation." He wrote in a strong hand, not too decipherable. He explained how fast traffic would be kept out of the sector — how dignity and peace, as he put it, would be restored to the pedestrian. "V3 roads, which go between the sectors, are for cars only, no pedestrians. There are eight bus stations around the edge of each sector, placed so that no one inside need walk more than twelve hundred feet." He paused. "This was a very big, important decision," he said gravely.

He picked up a yellow crayon. "The sector is a unit for habitation," he said, "so it needs to have a commercial unit." And with the yellow crayon he drew a line across his red oblong, continuing it so it crossed the next. It amounted to a picture of several bazaar streets laid end to end. "The commercial street," he said. "It is the main street of all the cities for a thousand years. A very lively street."

Then he took a green crayon and drew a line at right angles to the yellow one, through his red oblong. He continued this toward the top of the paper, and there he quickly sketched in the silhouette of some mountains. It was a diagram of the green strip, with the mountain view at its end. "Youth domain," he wrote beside it, again in lead pencil. "Schools, sports, et cetera." He said it was for the *moutons*, as he called them — the lambs, the children — to play on. "The slope of the site is perfect for irrigation," he said. "The water will come slowly down all the green strips, with small waterfalls."

He told me other things about the city, sketching as he did so. He even sketched a curve showing the twenty-four-hour rhythm of humanity, which he said was important in planning (it looked like an S lying down). And on the wall of his office he showed me other diagrams, more carefully done, which summarized the basic pursuits of man, like work, habitation and circulation, as they related to Chandigarh and the world. The room was full of theorizing, both visual and verbal — not to guess at the unexpressed theories in Corbusier's mind. He said the architecture on some Chandigarh streets would be controlled, and compared this to the Place Vendôme and the Rue de Rivoli in Paris, and to parts of Venice. And all the time he sketched. He discussed the industrial section, and the market section for meat and vegetables, which he drew in blue crayon. He said the city could not spread except by plan, and there would be no suburbs, just the urban and the rural — which I have since heard is a pet idea of his. He talked and sketched some more, and then I took my leave, and in taking it I asked how long he had needed to make the Chandigarh plan. "Oh, a very short time," he said. "Weeks only. Because all my life I had thought of it." And he had his faraway look as he shook my hand.

The Faqir of Ipi

THE FAQIR of Ipi has been renowned in his field — tribal
warfare on the Indian subcontinent's North-West Frontier — for more than three decades. His fame reached a
peak in the 1930s, when he led a major rising against the
British partly over a teen-age Hindu girl who had been
kidnaped, married to a Muslim and converted to his
faith; then recovered by the British, reconverted and
sent off to a new marriage in a Hindu zone. Muslims took
this as an offense against Islam, and by it and other issues
the Faqir inspired his Muslim tribesmen to hostilities that
tied down three British divisions, or so one hears now.
The trouble over the girl subsided in time, but the Faqir
continued fighting the British after it — as he had before
— in guerrilla war of varying intensity, waged from a
fastness in the hills, by the Afghan border. In 1947 the
British left India, and Pakistan claimed to be their heir
in the hills, but the Faqir has held that Pakistan cannot
inherit what the British did not possess. He has kept up

the fight from his lair, though on the issue of pure tribal autonomy now instead of religion, as all concerned are Muslims. In this fight he is counted among the leaders of "Pakhtunistan," a movement that he and other tribesmen — their common name is variously Pakhtun, Pushtun, or Pathan — seek to promote as a sovereign state in territory colored as Pakistan's on our maps. In this latest phase the Faqir is perhaps a more shadowy and mysterious figure than ever, since a thick cloud of propaganda has risen round him. Pakistanis pretend so far as possible that he and his movement don't exist, or, failing that, dismiss him as "just an old man in a cave," a puppet of Indian — and perhaps Russian — intriguers who pay him to make trouble. Afghans, on the other hand, whose territory adjoins the Faqir's and backs it up, treat him as a hero and his movement as a well-starred fight against oppression — the Afghan man in the street even talking of hypothetical Pakhtunistan as if it were a fact. These doubts and controversies taint the Frontier air, and they arouse the curiosity of one who travels, as I have recently done, between Pakistan and Afghanistan, the countries the Frontier separates. So when I had left Pakistan and been in Afghanistan awhile, I inquired if I could visit the Faqir, and in time a chance was given me.

The early details of this arrangement can't be divulged, but one August morning found me in southern Afghanistan riding a gray horse eastward toward the Pakistan, or Pakhtunistan, border in company with my son Chris, an Afghan friend named Rahman, and a handful of grooms and escorts who walked alongside, two of them leading pack horses. Rahman, whom I had met in Kabul, the Afghan capital, had wanted to visit Pakhtunistan himself and had undertaken to guide us. This was good luck, it turned out, for he was a man of parts — spirited and resourceful — and in mediating between us and our Pakhtun hosts did as fine a job as one could ask for in reconciling East and West. He was a Pakhtun himself, like many Afghans, and a devotee of the Pakhtun cause — he came from the nobility of a tribe some distance to our north, on the Afghan side of the line. He had lived abroad for many years, however, and was a master of English and of Western ways. He was about thirty-five and looked as if he had stepped from a Persian miniature, with dark curly hair, a dark mustache, an aquiline face and light-brown eyes — at times they seemed like amber. When we had started out he had been smartly dressed in a tweed jacket and gray flannels, but by now he wore the turban, full shirt and baggy trousers of a Pakhtun, which suited him better and better as we progressed and picked up dust, wear and tear.

We were riding up a narrow Afghan valley on this morning, with a low ridge to our left and a series of small irrigated fields to our right, along a stream. Many of these grew alfalfa, thick and rich green in color, which was now being harvested — I believe alfalfa began in that part of the world. At intervals we passed buff mud houses designed for the still lawless conditions of the region — with high walls, that is, unbroken except for gates

and crenelations, and with watchtowers at their corners.
I was impatient because we had a deadline for returning
and had already been much delayed, but even so our
party kept being slowed down by the footmen guiding
us, who repeatedly bade us wait in a grove or other rest-
ful spot while they sent someone up ahead. At last their
reason became clear. We heard faraway drums; we were
asked to dismount; and we walked forward round a bend
and were confronted, at some distance, by several dozen
armed men — a welcoming party of the Faqir's people —
drawn up in a row and awaiting us. We kept on walking
toward them, and as we did so they began firing sporadi-
cally into the air — rifles and pistols both they had, and
they shot them off with trigger-happy gusto. They
stopped when we reached the near end of their line, and
we were then introduced to three or four leading men
of the party, with whom we shook hands and exchanged
greetings. This ceremony was brief. In a few minutes we
were back on our horses and climbing the ridge to our
left. It was not high, and when we reached the top we
paused a moment. "Waziristan," one of our hosts said,
gesturing forward, and I gathered we were in the Faqir's
domain.

From that divide we traveled downward the rest of the
morning, about two hours, through a parched and glaring
mountain landscape — down a canyon, narrow at first but
widening, between slatelike rocks that shone like pewter
in the sun. The canyon was dry but for a tiny spring here
and there, and the slopes above were clad in tawny grass

— a Frederic Remington color — and dotted with tough green shrubs, like holly or live oak, which didn't give shade enough for a man to sit in. Lower down, as the morning wore on, we met a few goats grazing, but otherwise the scene was nearly lifeless, with the sun weighing on it.

Sometimes the drummers in our escort — there were two of them — beat their drums awhile, and the noise echoed stirringly amid the rocks. The escort numbered about sixty footmen under two or more khans — squires or nobles — who conducted us on horseback — the khans tended to fall in or out later on, but two stayed with us through the trip. Rahman told me that khans in this region never traveled without some armed retainers, and I gathered that our guard was honorary; though it was said that travelers in those parts dared not, for instance, camp at night in a pass without protection. These retainers with us had been raised from the countryside ahead for the occasion. They wore standard Pakhtun garb of turbans, long shirts and baggy trousers, in dim colors with an admixture of tattletale gray, for there was little spit and polish to them — they reminded me of our Continentals in *The Spirit of '76*. They wore belts, or bandoleers, of ammunition. They looked weatherbeaten. Their hair, usually black but sometimes henna-stained, was cut in bobs, a little shorter than the style we call "page boy." I gathered this was the rule with most Pakhtun tribes, and especially with the Wazirs and their neighbors the Mahsuds, whose country we were visiting.

All the men had leather sandals, but often they carried these in hand while walking on the rocks and gravel, I suppose to save them. They seemed as hard as men could be, and I have since heard Pakhtuns, or Pathans, ranked among the world's toughest warriors. They have fought each other, and outsiders, for centuries in their hills.

As we progressed, on foot and horseback, we saw sometimes a picket on a skyline up ahead, and he would fire some signal shots as we drew near. Once I made out such a figure on a peak high above us. He fired his shots and we rode in underneath him, out of sight. I thought it was the end of him — that he would be up there all day — but we rounded a bend and found him speeding down a steep spur to join us. He had gray in his beard, but he moved lithely over the boulders, and he showed no fatigue when he stepped down onto the path. Young and old, the Pakhtuns all seemed on this order as they led us through the wasteland.

At noon our canyon joined an easier valley, with a running stream and cultivation, and here we met our first house inside the Faqir's territory. It was a big two-storied one, of the usual dry mud, set high on the facing bank. The people there had been alerted to our coming, and several men stood out in front, firing their guns as we rode toward them on the gravel wash. The house, it turned out, belonged to one of our guiding khans — a slight, bearded, graying, thoughtful man — and we dismounted there and went inside, up a crude stairway to a guest room. It was an airy place, seeming very open for a Pakhtun house, with windows and a balcony overlooking the stream. Its walls were of smooth dry mud and its floors were covered entirely by rugs in Afghan patterns, of warm colors but with blues and blacks worked in.

This was the scene of our first Pakhtun hospitality in the Faqir's domain. We were brought tea as we reclined on the rugs. Clear sweetened green tea is the common Pakhtun beverage, though black tea is drunk too, often with milk. Each guest is given his green tea in a pot, and with it a bowl like a small Chinese rice bowl, in which has been put a liberal helping of sugar. He drinks from the bowl and keeps refilling it from the pot, and as he does so the sugar gradually dies out of the mixture — "going from sweet to the bitter," I have heard this called. So we sat resting in the khan's upstairs room, going from the sweet to the bitter and talking desultorily. People came and went. One was a henna-bearded ancient who turned out to be our host's father and who said he was ninety-seven, older than anyone he knew. He didn't join in the gathering much, but sat in a corner and told his Islamic beads. We idled thus for some time, and then two servingmen brought a white cloth like a tablecloth, laid it on the floor and began spreading on it what I soon came to know as the standard items of a Pakhtun feast — *polao*, or rice steamed with meat inside it; *kebab*, or meat broiled on spits; some smaller dishes of meat and vegetable stew; yoghurt; *nan*, or flat disks of unleavened bread; and finally fruit in season — in this case peaches and a melon. The bulk of the meat, here as in all Pakhtun feasts, was mutton, but it was varied with chicken too. The *kebab* might be made, as in American restaurants, of morsels run together on a spit, or it might be of big roasted chunks and bones. The meat in the *polao*, whether mutton or chicken, was normally in big pieces too, and you were supposed to tear it apart with your hands — Pakhtun or Afghan guests, indeed, were supposed to use their hands for everything, including rice, but foreigners, in view of their inexperience, were given plates and spoons. According to the theory, the host complimented his guests by providing them with a lavish feast, and they showed their appreciation — along with their happiness, their liking for the host, and so on — by eating of it in volume. I found it hard to make a really polite showing in this because the Pakhtuns had a huge capacity, and everyone fell to at once, so you were conspicuous only if you held back. Unless you made a dead set for bony pieces, and littered your place spectacularly, you were apt to be met in ten or fifteen minutes, when the pace died down, by remarks about your poor appetite. It was a real embarrassment of riches. I gathered that the Pakhtuns admired hearty eating and linked it with strenuousness in other lines, like fighting. They ate fast, too, with little formality, aside from pressing choice bits on the guests. Our meal that day was soon over, and servants brought us water for washing; then brought us tea; and we were left by our hosts in the guest room for a siesta. This lasted till five in the afternoon, for all our wish to hurry on — or, more exactly, our belief in the need to do so — and in the end we made only two or three further miles that day. We were suffering from an East-West conflict in our timing. We had set a date for returning to Kabul, which itself was keyed to faraway things like the reopening of school in America. The Pakhtuns, through their representatives, had agreed to this schedule, but I don't think they ever saw it as a weighty matter. I think Pakhtuns can move like a flash when concrete need arises — need, say, to head an enemy off at a pass — but I don't believe they are impressed by timetables as such. Now they had the countervailing obligation to guard us and treat us well — not only ourselves but the men and beasts with us — which required that we be fed properly and rested in the noon heat. I am sure that a couple of days' delay in our trip would have been small loss, in Pakhtun judgment, compared with the rudeness of passing us along too quickly. The theory of this was clear to us too, but a lifelong diet of alarm clocks is hard to overcome; and I chafed, and so did Chris, when a stated short halt threatened, as it often did, now and later, to stretch into many hours' dalliance. Luckily Rahman was there, and he grasped the problem and saw it through, now persuading the khans, now reassuring us, and in the end he got us back to Kabul almost on time.

At this stage, incidentally, Rahman was becoming steadily more of a Pakhtun in appearance and outlook, and was being accepted more and more by our Pakhtun hosts. The old man at this first house had known his grandfather, it turned out, and this improved his standing at once.

The short distance we covered that afternoon was in the same valley. For much of it we rode in the stream itself — it was wide and shallow, with a gravel bottom — while our escorts kept to paths on the bank; throughout the trip they often left us briefly, to take short cuts. At intervals the stream was edged by fields, and at the place where we stopped for the night, a mud-walled village, there was a wide expanse of these, mainly in rice. We strolled among them after leaving our horses, and the rice was a luminous jade green in the setting sun.

We did not walk through the village itself for fear of intruding on the women — in that country they were not wholly veiled, as in Kabul, but they were still modest and withdrawing in the Muslim way. Their costume, usually of dull black and dull red, always included a veil or shawl draped over their head, which they could hold across their face at will — showing only their eyes, perhaps. These eyes were generally lovely if one happened to glance at them while riding past, and I must say that veils add to the wearers' attractiveness, in the manner of women's clothes as a whole. But we were rarely close enough to see details. Except when drawing water the women stayed far from the trail — perhaps in their windowless mud courtyards, perhaps on the hills with their flocks. They were not seen praying in public, like the men. Orthodox Muslims are supposed to pray five times daily, and I believe the tribesmen did it faithfully. When we reached this village, for example, the men of our party all fanned out to separate places, made their ablutions, spread clean cloths upon the ground, and there did their obeisances toward the setting sun. I don't believe a non-praying man could amount to much in that society.

From talking with Rahman and the khans I gathered that the valley grew barley, rice and corn, though not enough to go round — the Faqir's holdings in general were not self-supporting, but had to get much grain from Afghanistan. This was partly paid for by small exports, they said, but mainly it was a gift, given out of the clannish sympathy of Afghans for Pakhtuns. They told me the Faqir's territory, known as Central Pakhtunistan, was one hundred by two hundred miles in extent; that North Pakhtunistan, farther up the border — not contiguous — was larger still; and that there was also much land in South Pakhtunistan. I couldn't check these figures and I presume the Pakhtuns were no stricter about them than about timetables. I do know there are certain bits of sovereign territory strung out on the Pakistan side of the border and calling themselves Pakhtunistan — nuclei of the dream nation their leaders talk of founding — but I can't define the limits of these. I can't even define the limits of the Faqir's holdings, which I visited. Looking at the map now I can place his own fastness, just inside Pakistan, but I believe that much of the space I crossed in getting there, while called Waziristan, was really Afghan soil as we understand it. I was told the Faqir controlled a band perhaps twice as wide on the other side, toward the Pakistan outposts, but I didn't see this. All I can say, really, is that he had a territorial basis in those mountains, comprising several valleys, and that these were peopled as herein described.

Rahman told me the village we were in — along with others like it — was supposed to send one man from every eight of fighting age to the Faqir's bodyguard, which actually, I gathered, was a sort of garrison for the region. These men were rotated, he said. Otherwise the male population stayed home and worked the fields except for emergencies or for occasions like the present, when a few dozen might be levied for escort duty. At work or play they kept their guns with them — as I constantly saw — and they could be called up at once, I was told, by prearranged drum or gun signals directed by the khan of the locality. These signals, according to Rahman, could tell them in which direction the danger lay — so they could go there without waiting to gather — and could also tell the degree of emergency, so that only one man from a family would drop his work, or two, or three, and so on. When parties of men were moving it was understood that villages along the way would feed them — as they were feeding us and our escort now — and each family knew its duty in this regard. Men were likewise fed by the community if in battle stations — food being brought there by the boys and extra men, or failing that, by the women. The women themselves, Rahman said, were well trained in cleaning guns, and could also use them if need be.

This mobilization scheme — and I don't know whether it was actually followed in most cases, or was more of an ideal blueprint — was described to me as we wandered by the fields and later as we settled down in the village's summer guest room, a plain mud-walled court open to the sky. (The winter guest room, a mud house, was near by, facing a yard where our horses were picketed and fed — the men of our escort slept at random in the open, guns beside them.) The ground of the guest court had been covered with rugs, and round these had been placed string beds for the khans and ourselves, with gay quilts. So the scene was colorful by daylight, and by night it became bright with stars overhead.

While idling there, awaiting our feast, we heard drums and war cries outside, and we went and found the men beginning a dance. The drums beat in a steady intricate rhythm, and the men gathered in a wide circle round them. They started dancing in a shuffle or skip, and the circle turned slowly. The men had guns and turbans on to start with, but in time they took them off and left them in a pile in the center. They danced faster. When they took their turbans off their bobbed hair hung free, and they made use of this in the dance by shaking their heads, and snapping and nodding them to the rhythm of the drums, so the hair swirled, standing out like that of golliwogs. Sometimes they sang in unison, melodies that Rahman said were Pakhtun love songs. And they made their wild cries, like rebel yells. Pairs faced each other in the circle, shaking their heads and clapping their hands.

They whirled. They danced crouching, like Cossacks. The drums speeded up and they ran in the circle, spinning and jumping.

After a while they stopped dancing for a spell of songs, or balladry. They sat round in a circle on the ground while one man stood in the middle singing old verses on tribal history, according to Rahman, and ad-libbing new ones on current affairs. Each stanza was followed by a refrain, with the circle joining in. Rahman translated a few stanzas, one of which went: "You might look at our ragged sleeves and be encouraged to fight a poor man, O Pakistan; but it is the hand that strikes, not the sleeve." Other stanzas were in like mood. Some were so bawdy that Rahman declined to translate them. I suppose a scholar would have related this singing to other schools of epic poetry or minstrelsy, and I understand that Pushtu, or Pashto, the Pakhtun tongue, is rich in verse, and well equipped for it.

In a while the dancing began again, the drums throbbing and the young men spinning, clapping and swirling their hair. They kept it up late, too, till after we guests had eaten our generous feast and gone to bed. I gathered that young Pakhtuns took pride in dancing all night, and the next day I saw some of those with us dancing along the trail when the drums happened to be beating. It was a real display of endurance. I gathered the tribesmen used it for this — for conditioning their bodies and showing the results. I suspected the dances did for them what the playing fields of Eton do for the British — taught the young men teamwork and hard usage of their muscles, while giving them a common thing to glory in. It seemed an essential part of tribal life, so Spartan in other ways too.

We left that place early, before sunrise, and started up a ravine toward another pass, dry and rocky like the last one — no land was green in that country, it seemed, without irrigation. We rode along, and I was less stiff in the saddle than I had expected; my horse had an easy, springy walk. We reached the summit, went down a dry ravine on the opposite side, and in time joined another easy valley like the one we had left. We traveled down the stream of this, passing fields now and then, and after rounding two or three bends we came to a mud village, a fair-sized settlement, where inevitably a new reception awaited us — a row of gun-shooting men this time *and* a tribal dance, its circle revolving spiritedly on the gravel — indeed the two were combined in a way, for the dancers shot their guns toward the sky as they leaped and whirled. Other men and boys stood round. It was a lively melee, and we were led through it by the khan of the place, a grave and self-effacing man with friendly eyes, who took us to his guesthouse.

As we sat drinking tea on the rugs there — going from the sweet to the bitter — he and our two accompanying khans began politely questioning me, through Rahman, about America and Pakhtunistan. Their ideas on our country, as one might guess, were respectful but vague, and a little apprehensive. They were concerned that we were giving arms to Pakistan, feeling these would be used against them, to which I could only answer that this was certainly not our intent so far as I knew, and that we bore Pakhtunistan no ill will — I could scarcely say, as Rahman pointed out, how few of us were aware of Pakhtunistan's existence.

The khans next regretted that Vice-President Nixon had done nothing for them as yet. He had received a Pakhtunistan delegation, they said, when in Kabul on his Asian trip last year, and had heard its story and promised to see what he could do. Rahman told me, aside, that a promise to see what one could do, if made by a khan himself, might soon result in drum or gun signals ordering men to arms, and he despaired of telling our hosts how differently the words should be taken when said by a Western statesman. I despaired too, thinking of "in" baskets, "out" baskets, Senators, Gallup polls and other complications so far away. I merely said that Vice-President Nixon, though a very important man, was but one of many who dealt with these questions; I said that everything took time, and consultation, and so forth and so on; and I let it trail off that way.

I stressed, of course, that I was not an official myself, and that what I said or did had no meaning where our policy was concerned. But I don't know what this accomplished. I understand that no other Western reporter had seen the Faqir of Ipi since the last World War, and I suppose the mere appearance of a Western face made its impression. I felt I was in the same plight here as our country itself — moving around in terra incognita and causing reactions that I did not intend and would never fully know about. Yet I could not see how to prevent this except by staying home.

The khans' good manners were enough to bridge the gulf between us, even if purely mental comprehension was not. We sat there and talked amicably while they pressed first tea on us, then later food. I was learning bit by bit about the Faqir, who was not referred to as such by his own people, incidentally, but as Haji Sahib. His actual name, I learned, was Mirza Ali. One could call him Mirza Ali Khan, the equivalent of Mr. Mirza Ali, or more respectfully one could say Haji Mirza Ali, signifying that he had made the haj, or pilgrimage, to Mecca. But among his followers Haji Sahib was enough — Sahib is a general honorific in those parts. Faqir is a Muslim term, Arabic to start with, used for a mendicant holy man; and Ipi, a Waziristan village, had been Mirza Ali's birthplace. He had been referred to as the Faqir of Ipi in the risings against the British, and this name had understandably taken hold in the press — as a world figure, such as he might be, he existed under no other.

Mirza Ali had been born sixty-six years ago, according to his followers, into the family of a khan of the Dawars, a small Pakhtun tribe allied with the Wazirs and Mahsuds. He had been given first-class religious training in the Muslim schools of the North-West Frontier, which had culminated in his pilgrimage to Mecca at thirty-one.

While he was on this his father had died, and he had been called home to take over the tribal responsibilities. It had so happened that this was in 1919, a year when the Afghans attacked the British, in the so-called Third Afghan War, with the Pakhtun tribes of Waziristan and elsewhere joining them. And it had happened further that there was a shortage of top men among the Wazirs, Mahsuds and allied tribes at the time, so the young Faqir had quickly succeeded to a wider leadership. He had not been schooled in warfare, of course, but he had shown himself generally gifted and, it appears, strongly anti-imperialist from his boyhood study and travels. He had soon made a name for resolution and for talent in guerrilla strategy. He had become leader of the war party in Waziristan, and as such had given the British, through the years, the trouble I had heard about. Now he was continuing the resistance against Pakistan, because she too was trying to crush the Pakhtuns' independence.

I inquired about the part of religion in the Faqir's struggle, but never got too satisfactory an answer. I sensed a wish to play the matter down, perhaps because the Faqir was no longer fighting infidels, perhaps because the whole idea, along with the name Faqir of Ipi, might give an impression of fanaticism — irrationality — distasteful to Westerners. I sensed this, as I say, but may be wrong; and I may be wrong, too, on the biographical details given above, which I dare say contain their share of legend. The Faqir was an enigmatic figure to me then, as indeed he still is, though I have seen him. But I believe his personality was strongly felt in these antechamber valleys, as we approached him.

From that village we rode on along the stream, bulging with our midmorning feast. Often, there and elsewhere, we met Pakhtun men in the trail, gun on back, and sometimes they joined us. *"Istrai mushai,"* we had learned to say on meeting — "May you not grow tired," that is, in the Pushtu language, which is reputed close to Aryan, as the Pakhtuns themselves are reputed close to Aryan stock. *"Istrai mushai,"* we would say, and shake hands in passing, a meeting of East and West not far from the scene of Kipling's ballad on that subject — for Kipling's border chief was himself a Pakhtun, or Pathan, and the landscape the colonel's son followed him over was related to this one, if not so high in the mountains.

We continued in the valley awhile and then began to climb another side canyon, which grew so steep that we dismounted and struggled up on foot, stopping often for a breather. We gained a high sharp ridge and looked out over a new valley, a brown pit in effect, with steep sides walling it on every hand. It was many hundred feet deep, perhaps more than a thousand, and I was told the Faqir's stronghold was in the bottom, though I could see nothing there yet — only a dry emptiness with a canyon running through. After resting we started downward on a zigzag path, walking quickly enough, with long strides, and in time we met a few men waiting on a spur. The chief of these was a Pakhtun elder, a solid-looking man, with reddish beard and blue eyes, who had come to welcome us on the Faqir's behalf. We shook hands with him and the others, then started down again, and we came in sight of a welcoming row of men, who soon were fusillading at the heavens. We did not stop, but kept on past them briskly till we found ourselves in a gully, a feeder of the main canyon. The crowd began to thicken there, men and boys beside us, waving and shooting. We ran a sort of gantlet for a while, people shooting on both sides. We were being swept along. We were between cliffs, and I noticed caves in them. We entered the main canyon, and it was a wider place, with a high cliff to our right and caves in this, some distance up. As we rounded the corner two small cannon began booming away. Men were dancing to drums. There was smoke, dust, color and movement in the sunlight, and much noise. We were taken up a long flight of dirt steps to a terrace, and thence into a cave, where we subsided in a cool hush. Pakhtun men brought us tea and then lemonade, and I discovered I was very hot and thirsty.

The cave had chairs, small tables and a big red Afghan rug covering the floor, which was about twenty feet square. I suppose it was a guest cave, for we spent the night there too, on string beds brought in. Its four walls sloped inward, and the corners between them were rounded, so that the whole tended toward a dome shape. The rock was what is called conglomerate — gravel mixed with hardened dirt — and the walls were rough, but they were nicely whitewashed. The cave had a cur-

tained bathing alcove in one corner, and next it was the
entrance, through which I gazed, out into the sunny air,
as we sat resting. An armed man always stood there, on
the terrace. And somewhere outside an internal-com-
bustion engine put-putted away in an odd falsetto.

The elder who had greeted us sat with us in the cave.
His name was Mohammed Zahir Shah, and I was told
he was the Faqir's "chief of internal affairs." The Central
Pakhtunistan Government — here located — had half a
dozen department heads like this, he said, together with
an advisory council, to the Faqir, of seventeen men, and
a representative assembly of one hundred and two. Again,
I don't know how closely these forms and figures were
observed, but I understand that Pakhtuns in general mix
a lot of simple mountain democracy with the khans'
paternalism. Others sat with us in the cave too. One was
a good-looking young man named Ramazani, citified in
his dress for a Pakhtun, who was introduced as the son of
a big Mahsud leader killed in the British troubles. He
was the head of the representative assembly, I was told,
and the chief of publicity.

We talked and rested, and after enough of this we
learned we still had time to kill before our meeting with
the Faqir, which was scheduled for four o'clock. We
went outside and looked around, soon swept along by a
sea of Pakhtuns, who took us from cave to cave. The
engine, it turned out, was in an armory cave, where they
said they made grenades, small arms and ammunition.
Another cave had a little printing press. A third, very

deep, had sacks of flour. I didn't count the caves, but I suppose there were a dozen or two in all, used variously for living, working and storage. In conception the place — it was named Gurwik — reminded me of Yenan, the old Chinese Red capital — likewise a cave-rimmed fastness in barren hills — but it was infinitely narrower and on a smaller scale. It had little shelter but the caves themselves — just a few buildings on the terraces, one of which was pointed out as the Faqir's place of prayer. I saw a few hundred men in the canyon now, but was told the caves could take thousands if need be.

One thing shown us was a scar high on the cliff, where a British bomb had chipped off a big piece of stone. The British had tried hard, I gathered, to bomb the Faqir out, but with no success. He was still ready for air attack, it seemed. As we walked round I heard several bursts from a machine gun somewhere on the cliffs.

Our interview was held on the terrace of the Faqir's cave, and it was unusual, as interviews go, because the Faqir himself did not do the talking, but left this to Mohammed Zahir Shah, who sat beside him on a string bed along with a third man, one of the Faqir's relatives. The bed had two brocaded silk cloths on it — one red, one green — over a white cotton mattress, and the Faqir sat on these with his legs folded before him. He was slight of body and had a thin face — brown, sunburned, ascetic — even spiritual, I should say — with many small lines in it. His sparse black beard was streaked with gray. His turban was peach colored, and over it was draped a pale-green cotton cloth like a shawl. He wore a khaki tunic, a bandoleer of ammunition, a khaki waistcoat and baggy gray Pakhtun trousers. He was very quiet as he sat there, his brown eyes gazing somewhere else, and he seemed indrawn; yet his presence was compelling. Rahman and I were seated at a small table near the bed, with two bright bouquets on it in tumblers. Then round us all stood and sat a circle of the Faqir's armed, turbaned followers — perhaps thirty men in the front row — and they were rapt and spellbound, still as the brown cliff overhead. Twice there were interruptions, and the Faqir stopped them by raising a single finger, in silence. Twice he moved his legs slightly on the bed, and I believe everyone was sharply aware of this. There was an air of crystal concentration throughout the interview, which lasted half an hour. The Faqir seemed withdrawn indeed — fatigued even, as if from a long vigil — but he closely followed what was said, and three times he was moved to add something, talking in a murmur barely audible.

The words themselves were not impressive, though they came in volume from Mohammed Zahir Shah. He had been over the ground beforehand with the Faqir, I was told, and what he said plainly had the latter's approval. But I doubted if it had his style, which I felt would be economical, and surely aimed. Then each answer was deftly summarized, rather than translated, by Rahman, so what I got in the end was akin to history — a terse account of the event at long remove — and I shall not repeat much of it here.

I asked about the guiding idea of the Faqir's movement, and was told it was freedom. His people, I was told, had not been conquered by Genghis Khan or by anyone since — a proud boast, in those much fought-over mountains, but I think a true one; they had not been conquered by the British, and they did not mean to be conquered by the Pakistanis, whom they regarded as just some more outsiders bent on changing them. It was at the end of this answer — a long one in its delivery — that the Faqir spoke, or murmured, for the first time. He repeated that freedom was the principle, and then was silent.

I was told other things at length — about America, for instance, and Pakhtunistan, and the offenses of Pakistan — and the freedom motif kept recurring in the pattern. The Faqir — it was explained to me — thought the British had been less dangerous than Pakistan because everyone had known they would go home in time — they had even known it themselves. But Pakistan was on the ground to stay, and in the end she sought to smother the Pakhtuns culturally.

Some flies hovered about the Faqir as his spokesman talked, and an old tribesman behind him waved them away, silently and unbidden, with a leafy branch; and there seemed to be devotion — affection — in the Faqir's relationship with this man and the others in the circle.

The British, I was told, had had their on seasons and off

seasons, dependably, in fighting the tribesmen of this region. But Pakistan had shown she might strike any time — she used both military and economic weapons — and this kept up the strain, so there was no rest. It was growing unbearable, and even now the Faqir was considering whether to seek a desperate remedy and go really on the warpath. His advisers had urged this, I was told, but the Afghan Government, his supporter, had urged against it, and now the decision lay with him.

I took this to be a warning, which I was meant to convey to the outside world. But at the moment I saw the statement chiefly as a way of drawing the Faqir into the interview, and I asked him through Rahman to tell us how he might decide the matter. Some of his men joined in this too, leaning forward eagerly and begging him to speak. But he shook his head and murmured that he wouldn't.

The talk went on, with explanations of how Pakhtunistan, if carved from Pakistan, could be a workable country, and how the people wanted it. Meanwhile the Faqir sat silent under the silent cliff, with his men around him, and one could have heard a pin drop. At length we were told it was almost half past four, the time for prayer, and the interview must end. We were given presents — some Pakhtun embroidery and an Afghan dagger each. The Faqir spoke for the third time, saying many of the Pakhtun khans were in Gurwik now — for a gathering in the next day or two — and they would welcome us to visit their homes later if we could manage it. Then he

rose. He moved stiffly, and I have since been told he had
lumbago. He said good-by to us gently and we left, a
way opening for us through the thronged Pakhtuns.

To speak for myself, I felt elated after the interview.
I felt I had had the frustration one is supposed to get
when visiting oracles — that the voice had been muffled
and diverted by its crew of managers, and twisted almost
past recognition. But I felt that the oracle itself was gen-
uine — that there had been something there, albeit intangible. The Faqir's spell on those around him, and the
concentration in his presence, had been extraordinary. I
cannot analyze it, or explain his gentleness in relation to
the warring spirit of his people, in which he seemed so
great a factor. Later Rahman — a believer — was taken to
the Faqir's place of worship. He told me he saw a
Pakhtunistan flag there and some verses in Arabic and
Persian. One of the latter he translated for me as follows:
"It is a good custom left behind to us from those who
loved deeply, and whom we should love for their love, to
die and plunge into blood for the sake of one's love." I
don't know how much this explains. I have heard that
the Persian poets meant something very big by love —
love of God, or love of all creation — and I would dare
to guess that the Faqir — like this poet with his love and
bloodshed — saw something transcendental, besides mere
gunfire itself, in the Pakhtuns' struggle, which gave it
meaning, and that his followers sensed this. But I couldn't
prove any such thing.

After the interview I went back to the terrace by our

cave, and I was left alone there while I sat and wrote some notes. It was growing dusky in the closed-in canyon. I was in a bay of this, I realized — buttresses stuck out on either side of me, at some distance, and they too had caves and terraces, as did the main wall behind me. Several terraces had string beds on them. The canyon itself was like a square trough, a couple of hundred feet across by a couple of hundred feet deep. I saw men down below on the gravel floor, standing in knots, talking — having said their prayers. A flock of goats was being held there. A stream ran on the gravel bed, and I could hear it babbling; and short of it a few irrigated patches grew corn and squash. Upstream two camels were tethered, I noticed, and as I watched them a big band of men — several dozen — appeared from that direction, coming round a bend. They had drummers with them, beating out a rhythm, and they were dancing; and they shot their guns in the air as they passed. Then they disappeared round the bend downstream. I found out later they had come to join the gathering the Faqir had mentioned.

After they were gone it was quieter, and getting darker. There were some horses on the canyon's other side, where the ground began sloping up to the cliff, and they whinnied now and then. Goats bleated. A donkey lay down on the gravel with deliberation. Looking up from my notes once, I observed that the cliff opposite, while nearly vertical, was broken by vegetation, and that goats were wandering and grazing on the steep face. I reflected that Pakhtuns would probably venture on it

too, and just then I saw a Pakhtun girl, in a red dress
with black trimmings, starting up it. She was the only
woman I was to see at Gurwik. She went quickly and
deftly up the sheer rocks after the goats, a feat that I
ruled out for myself even in imagination.

It grew darker, and the men down below prayed
again, spreading their cloths on the gravel. Then they
went back to standing round in knots. One man caught
a goat by the hind leg and took it away. Another band
of newcomers came trooping in from upstream, shouting
their rebel yells, drumming, dancing and firing in the air.
It was so dark now that the flashes of their guns stood
out plainly. They too went round the corner out of
sight, and after that it was too dark to write more
notes.

Rahman, Chris, Mohammed Zahir Shah, Ramazani and
some others came up, and in time a feast was laid for us
on the terrace. We sat and ate it by lamplight, with
darkness for a background, and as we did so Rahman
confessed to being very moved. "I have always wanted
to be a Pakhtun guerrilla," he said, "and fight for something worth while. That is better than sitting at a desk
for money, isn't it?" I agreed, and I wondered who
would not at that moment.

The feast ended, and later we went down onto the
gravel and watched a dance — a more spectacular one
than ever, for the men lit a bonfire in the circle, and it
threw big shadows of the leaping, whirling dancers on the
cliff. I think Rahman stayed up late that night, talking

with guerrillas in their caves. But I went to bed early and slept.

The next morning we started back at seven, departing from another dance on the canyon floor — much dust being thrown up in the sunshine — and making farewells at various stages on the slope. I was pushed up the last steep part of this by a huge Pakhtun — he was my senior in years, I guessed, and he was beefy, with a great red face and twinkling blue eyes. He pushed me vigorously for scores of yards — really tough going — but I did not hear him breathe.

We went back the way we had come, through the two valleys and the pass between them. We traveled faster now, with but one stop for feasting, as Rahman had made a compact with our hosts. As we went along, the sun climbed higher and the rocks baked hotter, and the men with us must have felt this keenly, but they walked on with a will. I mused about their freedom, which the Faqir had dwelt on so. Freedom they had all right, I felt, but it was freedom with discipline — freedom conditioned on their forcing their muscles, and bearing the sun, and risking a hostile bullet in some pass — freedom really, when you boiled it down, to be a Pakhtun, and not much else. If a Pakhtun youth preferred less manly ways, I wondered, would he be free to follow them? And the women — would not some of them choose supermarkets, and television, if free to do so? I could imagine these questions in my head, but there was no hint of them in what I saw around me. All I saw was a line of tough men and boys walking on the flinty path, demonstrating the mountain virtues at their best, as their fathers had done since the time of Genghis Khan — say A.D. 1200 — and before. They walked through the glare, and sometimes one of them would show the virtue of generosity by offering me fruit from the folds of his clothing — small mountain pears or peaches, it might be, that he had carried all this way. I would take the gift and wonder how I really stood with the giver — as friend or otherwise. I wasn't thinking so much of a political conflict — between slogans of Pakhtunistan and Pakistan — but of a larger one: the conflict of the machine age against spice and variety in human life. I should note that I had been aware of this struggle before coming to the Faqir's domain, or to Afghanistan. I had seen the Pakhtuns, or Pathans, of the Pakistani lowlands, and had been struck by how they were adapting themselves to modern times, to roads and schools and radios — were becoming like the world-wide man-in-the-street, instead of wild mountaineers. I had then felt that this modernism was spreading outward through the hills from the Pakistani valleys, and now in fact I was seeing the same movement, from the receiving end, as the Faqir's guest. So as I ate the Pakhtuns' fruit I reflected that as an American I belonged to this machine age that threatened their treasured ways. But I didn't see that I could stop its spread to please them, or that I should even try. I could only pray that harmony might ease their meeting with it.

We rode through the two valleys, and over the pass between them, making our single stop for food and rest. Sometimes Pakhtun houses by the way gave us buttermilk from earthen jars, and this was most refreshing. The day passed on, and around the four-thirty prayer time we finished with the second valley and started up the canyon into the Faqir's bordering wasteland. It was hard going again for our escort, and when we came to the little springs the men would drink from them, and cool their feet in the overflow if possible. The climb grew steeper, and the small gray-bearded khan who was leading us dismounted and gave his horse to an older man. We reached the divide at dusk, and we rested there a moment, but soon we pressed on, down into the Afghan valley while darkness fell. We didn't have much farther to ride. The jeep that had brought us to these parts had managed to come up the valley in our absence, on a patched-up road, and after a mile or two we found it, and we said good-by there to the khans and their retainers, though we could not see their faces.

We tried to drive back to Kabul that night, but got lost and ran out of gas, and ended by sleeping through the small hours on a desert, and not making our goal till early afternoon. Rahman saw us through these crises with more spirit and resources than ever, and I came to feel he probably *should* be a Pakhtun guerrilla. At Kabul Chris and I stayed but a few hours, traveling from there posthaste back to Pakistan and down through that country to its seaport capital of Karachi, where he made his split-second plane appointment in good time.

As for me, I am still in Karachi, where the Faqir of Ipi and his movement have a different existence from the one I saw. Here they exist as an abstract legal and political question, about which much has been written — pro and con — by Afghans, Pakhtuns and Pakistanis. The claims conflict and the points are subtle, and I feel it is better to leave them to fate and politicians, and not to thrash them out here in their complexities. I don't know what will happen to Pakhtunistan, except that it is an open question still; but I hope it will be settled thoughtfully, for real people with real feelings are concerned. That is one trouble. In coming away from a remote place like the Faqir's mountains one always meets with a law of diminishing reality. People who have been real and vivid in the hinterland are treated increasingly as paper abstractions — paper dolls indeed — as one emerges into so-called civilization. In Karachi I have sensed a tendency to do this with the Faqir's men. So I here report clearly, at least, that they are not paper dolls.

Tenzing

DARJEELING's best-known citizen, Tenzing Norkay, is in residence now, though unseasonably, for the year's climbing has begun and most of his Sherpa colleagues are off helping Westerners up the peaks. His presence reflects the change in his affairs since May 29 last year, when he and Edmund Hillary stood on Mount Everest. That fact earned him a rest from his climbing career, which had been arduous, and it plunged him into a new world of contracts, publicity and politics that he can't easily withdraw from and that keeps him under a strain of adaptation. Not only, like many famous men, is he unschooled in publicity's ways; he also deals but haltingly in English, its lingua franca. Just to keep track of his own new life, therefore, demands hard concentration. Tenzing complains of having lost twenty-four pounds since climbing Everest and says — if not really meaning it — that he wouldn't have done so had he foreseen the results. His troubles are compounded by an ele-

ment of jealousy in Darjeeling — of a prophet without
honor in his country — of a disagreement whether he
should be called a great man or only an able servant. He
is sensitive and often feels this. "I thought if I climbed
Everest whole world very good," he says at such times.
"I never thought like this." Yet he carries on with modesty and grace. The modesty is a trait remarked on by
most observers. Tenzing is at everyone's disposal. He
has fixed up a small museum in his Darjeeling flat, with
his mountaineering things, his trophies, and pictures of
his climbs and triumphs, and he is available there to all
comers from ten in the morning to half past four in the
afternoon. As a rule he wears Western clothes with an
Alpine flavor — perhaps a bright silk scarf, a gray sweater,
knee-length breeches, wool stockings and thick-soled
oxfords, well polished. These suit him, for to an American visitor, at least, he seems like an Oriental version of
a European film star. He is a handsome man, sunburned
and well groomed, and he has a radiant — ever friendly —
smile with gleaming white teeth. One feels that his presence, and style of broken English, if faithfully conveyed
on the screen, would have much the same effect as Mau-
rice Chevalier's or Charles Boyer's. Redolent with this
charm Tenzing stands duty at his museum each morning
and afternoon, putting up with tourists of all nations. He
listens intently to their idle questions, phrased in all the
accents of English, and answers as best he can, often
laughing in embarrassment. With or without Mrs. Tenzing, he poses for snaps on his balcony — some visitors

attack him with two cameras, still and movie. And he loses money by it rather than gaining, for he gives each caller a signed photo of himself and takes contributions only for a charity, the Sherpa Climbers' Benevolent Fund. He seems to look on the ordeal as a duty, to the Sherpa people and to India, among other things, a feeling in which he is encouraged by those near him. The other day I, who have been bothering him too, remarked in wonder on how many people he receives. "If I don't," he answered, "they say I am too big." And he scratched his head and laughed nervously.

Tenzing's nationality was in doubt when he rose to fame, and this caused hard feeling between India and Nepal, which was the land of his birth and scene of the Everest climb. When he flew to England with the Everest party he took passports of both countries, and even now he says he doesn't know how to dress — if he wears Indian clothes he offends Nepal and vice versa. But it is pretty well settled that he is a man of Darjeeling, India, through choice and long residence, though Nepalese by birth and Sherpa — really Tibetan, that is — by stock. This mixture, odd as it may sound, is actually common, for the Sherpas long ago migrated from the high Tibetan wastes to those of Nepal — along the Everest slopes — and in this century many further migrated to Darjeeling, a British resort that offered work for coolies, porters and guides. Perhaps a hundred Sherpa families live in Darjeeling now, and Tenzing Norkay, or Tenzing Norkay

Sherpa, trod a well-worn path when he came here in 1933. This spelling of his name, incidentally, is the one he now approves and uses on his cards, though "Tensing" and "Norkey" have also had currency. All are unscientific, I am told by a European anthropologist here, a scholar of Tibetan. He says Tenzin Norgyä would be a better phonetic rendering by approved rules, and transliteration from the Tibetan spelling would give bsTan-aDzin Nor-rGyäs. But Tenzing Norkay has probably won. The Sherpas don't use surnames as we know them. Tenzing means "thoughtholder" or "thoughtgrasper." Norkay means "increasing wealth." Both are given names. Sherpa is a caste or clan name, a common thing in these parts. It plays a little, but not quite, the same role in Tenzing Norkay Sherpas as "Bostonian" might in George Apley Bostonian — or "Yankee" in George Apley Yankee.

The Sherpas, Darjeeling and Mount Everest are a triangle that has framed Tenzing's life. Darjeeling is a hill station — a "Paradise of Hill Resorts," the guidebook calls it — seven thousand feet high on the Himalayas' south slope. The terrain all round is steep, and landslides are common. For decades people came up here by a small mountain train, a marvel of the time and — to quote the guidebook again — the "costliest railway in the world." You can come here now by auto, corkscrewing up a steep road amid terraces of tea bushes, but the train still runs; its toy-size red cars and green locomotive chug in and out of the bottom of town, and its tootings embellish the day. Darjeeling itself is plastered in the curve of a steep hillside. Some streets are level, running along the hill's face, and these are linked by others like zigzag ramps, or by steps. It is a small place and each man knows what his brother is doing; often they meet while doing it. The town gazes out on a void, and from afar the blocks of its buildings look like horizontal strips pasted on a screen. Tenzing's flat is in a pink stucco house on the highest of the level streets, now called Gandhi Road in his part, and Nehru Road farther on. Like most of Darjeeling it has a fine view, on clear days, of snowy peaks to the northwest. They appear to float in the blue-gray emptiness, and they sparkle majestically. The main one in that view is Kanchenjunga, the world's third highest. To see Everest itself you must go to a nearby lookout called Tiger Hill.

The British made Darjeeling into a refuge from the heat of Calcutta, their main Indian port — both are in Bengal, in India's northeast corner. The Bengal Government came here for the hot months, as did wives and children of businessmen; or children alone, to attend the boarding schools that sprang up. Hotels were built and filled, and natives converged to serve as cooks, waiters, grooms or merchants, according to their talent. The Sherpas, hardy rather than urbane, drew outdoor jobs. For a while Tenzing, still a youth when he came here, rented a pony to the Sahibs and their children on the Chowrasta, Darjeeling's main square. Mrs. Tenzing, born in Darjeeling of Sherpa parents, often worked before last year at menial jobs like porterage. Sherpas women porters are seen on the streets here today, with baskets on their backs like big inverted cones or pyramids. They are smallish with Mongoloid features — flat noses and high cheekbones — and they wear braids and heavy jewelry.

Aside from tea the resort business was Darjeeling's main economic point, and times have changed. Business held up all right during the war, one hears, for British and American officers came here on leave and did the things, like trekking in the hills, that Darjeeling was set up for. But now it is different. The Bengal Government is Indian and does not come here. Some hotels and many villas are closed. Such tourists as Darjeeling draws are apt to be Indians, who keep fewer servants and do less trekking, or Americans, who have a new sort of timing. It is common now for Americans to whiz round the world by plane. This takes them through Calcutta, as a rule, and if they like they may get off there and whiz up to Darjeeling. But they rarely do more than spend a few nights in the echoing Hotel Mount Everest, take some shots of Tenzing, glimpse the snows if they are lucky — or shiver in the mists if not — and then whiz back. It isn't the same thing.

There are still a number of British people in Darjeeling, some living in retirement, and they are beset by inflation and change. Costs here are said to be three times those of the thirties, and there are labor troubles in the tea gardens. I have been told of violence done to British planters by native workers with little or no punishment, which is neither conducive to order nor in the old British style. In this atmosphere one would expect to hear complaints that Tenzing is being spoiled, and one does.

The other evening I was walking on Gandhi Road near his place, and I met three or four people coming toward me. Two dogs rushed out in the darkness and barked at them.

"Tenzing's dogs," said a lady's voice.

"Has he got *dogs* now?" said a man as if discovering the limit of vanity.

To us Darjeeling is a simple place, but to Sherpadom it is the great world. Sherpa boys run away to it as others run away to sea; Tenzing did this himself. From Darjeeling the Sherpa country sounds remote and almost unreal. Sherpa means "man — or men — from the east" in Tibetan. East of where is not certain, but the Sherpas' present locale is clear enough. It is in northeast Nepal, just south of the Tibetan border — on the edge, that is, of the Tibetan plateau. The plateau covers much of Central Asia, at a great height, and part of its southern edge is fenced by peaks, including Everest. Once past them the ground falls sharply toward the plains of India, and for five hundred miles, west to east, this slope is called Nepal — Nepal shows on the map as a long shape adjoining the plateau's rim. The Sherpa country is a splotch in its northeast corner, generally over ten thousand feet high, sometimes nearer twenty. Its main village — a few rows of stone Tibetan houses — is called Namche Bazar, which probably means Big Sky Market. Tenzing's mother lives there now; she is old, and in photographs has a wrinkled but lively face. The Sherpas are close to nature. They raise yaks, which thrive on their blizzardy pastures and thin air, and they grow potatoes in favored spots; in one of these, a Sherpa woman revealed here the other day, people know it's time to begin planting when a nearby waterfall thaws. Another element in their surroundings is the Abominable Snowman, or Yeti, a still partly mythical creature that walks like a man and leaves tracks to baffle Everest climbers. Many Sherpas in Darjeeling report having seen the Snowman, though Tenzing does not. "With my eyes I never seen," he says, "only footprint, very much big, one foot long." And he gestures with his hands. Some here think the Snowman is supernatural, and the sight of it will kill you. Others maintain it is a variety of bear or ape that will be tracked down sooner or later, like the giant panda.

Most Sherpas have an impulse to leave their difficult homeland. One way of escaping is to turn trader and run yak caravans over the high passes into Tibet, perhaps settling down there in the end — there is said to be a colony of Sherpa traders in Lhasa, the Tibetan capital. Another escape, of course, is Darjeeling, about twenty days' walk from Namche Bazar, across the India-Nepal border. Young Sherpas come here, work, go back, bring a family, work, go and leave the family, come back, go again, and so forth. When the men first come to Darjeeling they are apt to be gotten up in the Tibetan way, with long braided hair and huge earrings, but they soon shed these and don't appear in them again. Women, on the other hand, cling to the Tibetan style — it can be seen in Mrs. Tenzing's pictures — with its coiled braids, plain dark dresses and striped woolen aprons; the stripes are narrow and in many colors, and they suggest the bands of a spectrum. The feminine dress varies in detail — depending partly on new twists in Lhasa, the high-altitude Paris — but to the untrained eye it is uniform.

Here at Darjeeling most Sherpas live in a neighborhood called Tung Soong Bustee, a collection of poor houses done mainly in corrugated iron. It is over the hill from the main town and looks east, which means it has no view of the snows; but it can be cheerful after sunrise — as I learned the other morning — when the rest of town is still buttoned up. I set off before seven that morning to have a look. I walked along Nehru Road to the Chowrasta — the plaza — which lies in a saddle of the ridge. A few Sherpa men and women had come there already with small ponies — chestnut, piebald and gray — that they would rent later if customers showed up. They were sluicing them down with water, brushing them, and picking out their hoofs. From there I hairpinned back on the ridge's other side, along what had once been Calcutta — but now is Tenzing Norkay — Road. It was of dry hard dirt, with cobbles in some stretches, and it ran level across the hill face. It shone in the sun. I walked along, gazing down the steep to my left and passing houses scattered in the brush there, with zigzag paths, and soon I looked on the buildings where Tenzing had form-

erly lived — he had shared one room there with his wife
and two daughters, right up to his Everest success. I saw a
cluster of tin roofs with pigeons on them, and a dovecote
in the end of the biggest one. A dozen prayer flags rose
round them here and there, tall strips of cloth attached to
bamboo poles; the strips were white originally, but gray
with the columns of prayers — thousands and thousands
of words — stamped on them. They gleamed as the sun
shone through; and they flapped in the breeze and set up
good vibrations that would spread far and wide, according to Sherpa belief, which is Tibetan Buddhist. There
wasn't much activity round the buildings; but a few
women with braids, high cheekbones and the small square
Sherpa build were drawing water from a public tap on
the road near me, in pails and old kerosene tins. Down
below the roofs the world fell away to a valley where I
knew there were tea gardens; but I couldn't see them now
for there was a haze there, and the sun shone on it and
made the place seem infinitely deep, like Shamlegh Mid-
den in *Kim*. Crows skimmed over it far below, and on the
roofs the pigeons cooed.

While I gazed I heard hoofbeats and was hailed, and
I turned and there was Tenzing, out for a ride. He rode
a brown pony, wore English-style boots over khaki
trousers, and used an English saddle, but with a bright
Tibetan rug. He had a red wool cap on his head. He
stopped and chatted a moment, smiling in all his open-
ness. The pony was just under thirteen hands, brown, fit
and well groomed; he said it came from Tibet and showed

me a brand on its hindquarter that looked like a Chinese character. He talked a moment in the warm sun, then trotted off, and I went back to breakfast, passing some garrulous Sherpa women on the way.

The triangle's third leg, Mt. Everest, has been a British institution since the First World War, or at least the resolve to climb it has. Long before that it was known as the world's highest mountain — since 1850, when it was measured by triangulation from the Indian plains, by sightings over Nepal. The news was a surprise, for Everest — modest itself — does not stand out in the naked eye above the peaks around it. Since then it has always been rated highest despite threats from flash contenders like Amne Machin in northwest China, and despite arguments over the exact figure. The Survey of India called it 29,002 feet, admittedly an approximation. For a while this was nearly supplanted by 29,149 — the result of later sightings — which got on American Air Force maps, among others, but in the main 29,002 has prevailed, on the ground that no sighting is reliable, and it is better to choose one and stay with it. The peak was named early in the game for Sir George Everest, a Survey of India man who had retired in 1843, and this stuck despite local names advanced then or later — the Tibetans call it Chomolungma and a Survey pamphlet mentions, among others, Mi-ti Gu-ti Cha-pu Long-nga, meaning "You cannot see the summit from near it, but you can see it from nine directions and a bird that flies as high as the summit goes blind." Since Indian independence, and especially since last year, there has been further agitation to rename it, with "Tenzing" put forth as one candidate; but little has come of this.

The British attack on Everest was spearheaded in the early twenties by a few men like George Leigh Mallory, who disappeared near the summit and who gave "Because it is there" as his reason for wanting to climb it. These early tries launched what has been called a Thirty Years' War on Everest, with Britain's young manhood increasingly called into play — not to mention her diplomatic connections, the funds of her banks, and other of her resources. Sir John Hunt's book on the 1953 climb acknowledges help from a six-page list of firms, individuals and government agencies, nearly all British; his expedition's sponsor was the Duke of Edinburgh; and all in all the venture was a national one.

A custom has developed in Himalayan climbing whereby different nations take on different peaks, which avoids confusion. At this writing American, French and Japanese parties have already entered the mountains, and more are expected. Each is headed neatly for a different goal (the American group — the California Himalayan Expedition — is out to climb Makalu, a 27,800-foot peak in Everest's near vicinity). In the division of mountains the British took Everest, and they are the only nation that has really assaulted it excepting the Swiss, who tried twice in 1952, along with Tenzing. Between the wars Britain would probably have had it to herself anyway, for she was the only Western country on speaking terms with Tibet. In those days Nepal would not admit climbing parties, and Everest could be approached only by the Tibetan, or north, face, a condition that has since been reversed. By 1951 Tibet was forbidden again to all Westerners, for the Reds were dominant there, but meanwhile Nepal had opened up. Now the peaks' south faces get the traffic.

When the road lay through Tibet, Darjeeling made a natural jump-off spot, for it was near the caravan track from India to Lhasa and had good rendezvous facilities. Climbers could assemble here, start breathing mountain air, check their equipment and, if newcomers, learn something of the Himalayas. Darjeeling received them warmly. Some parties stayed at the Planters' Club, in the top center of town, above where Gandhi and Nehru Roads now meet (but then they were Auckland Road and Commercial Row). The club's terrace has a fine view of the snows, and an expedition, before setting out, could be blessed there, with Sherpas and all, by lamas from the nearby monastery of Ghoom. The Sherpas fell naturally into the setup. Their worth as high-altitude porters had been discovered at the start of this century by A. M. Kellas, a British mountaineer, and thenceforth they were in the game at all levels, from carrying picnics to supplying base camps. Sherpas have helped in all serious attacks on Everest and other high peaks in this stretch of the Himalayas, though a German party did without them last year when climbing Nanga Parbhat, in the range's west end. Nanga Parbhat is now in Pakistan, whose red tape vis-à-vis India is too inflamed for Sherpas to pass through it.

This is a new experience for them, incidentally. All this century they have drifted innocently across the otherwise stern borders of Tibet and Nepal. If peaks were forbidden it was not to Sherpas, but to their Western employers — though this amounted to the same thing, really, for Sherpas did not aspire to climb mountains by themselves. To them it was a livelihood, made possible by Western whim; and the profit motive is central to the picture of a Sherpa in the Western climber's mind. In this picture the Sherpa is a likable chap: hardy, loyal to death, experienced in things like frostbite care; but childish, mercenary and needing to be led. The child side appears in climbers' tales of Sherpas' hiding rocks in each other's packs, or blowing their pay on *chang*, the Tibetan beer. Hunt's account of being delayed at Namche Bazar on his way back from Everest is a version of the picture; his Sherpas caroused and were blind to his haste.

As the climbing game grew it was co-ordinated by the Himalayan Club. (By and large, the club uses the sound Himaláyan, the third syllable rhyming with gray. Indians call the range Himahlyuh, and the English spelling Himalaya was meant to convey this. But the attempt was too pedantic for the common man, who clutched at the pronunciation Himaláya and made it prevail in English usage.) The Himalayan Club helps climbers with advice and services, including the recruitment of Sherpas. Much of its business is handled in Darjeeling by the secretary, a British planter's wife, who keeps files on more than a hundred Sherpas, listing their records, qualities and vital statistics. Sherpas start reporting to her early in the year so they can have jobs by March, when the climbing season begins. Often they walk here from Namche Bazar for the purpose. The club assigns them tasks it deems suitable, from sirdar down — a sirdar is a foreman; the same word is used in Darjeeling tea gardens. Tenzing is an old sirdar of the club — and went as such with Hunt in 1953 — though he is now outside it. The club is the hiring hall, traditionally, and Darjeeling is the place for such activity, though climbing parties actually start out from Nepal now. Sometimes they fly to Katmandu, the Nepalese capital, and sometimes they go in overland from the Indian plains. Their Sherpas — the principal ones at least — are sent to meet them from Darjeeling by prearrangement, even if it takes a fortnight's walking. Thus the machine has grown up.

Tenzing was born in the machine. His childhood home was a village called Thami, near Everest and about fourteen thousand feet high. His father owned yaks, and as a boy Tenzing herded them, often in pastures thousands of feet above Thami itself. He also went on caravan trips over Nanpa La, a nineteen-thousand-foot pass by Everest's west shoulder. From the start he was as near Everest as a human could be. Two legends about him — one religious, one Horatio Alger, both perhaps true — have begun. After his descent in 1953 he said to James Burke of *Life* that the monks of Thyangboche Monastery, in the Sherpa country, had told him the "Buddha God" lived on Everest, and he had always hoped to climb it and worship there. His offering on the summit — of a chocolate bar, biscuits and lollypops — is well known, and there was much news of him in this vein last year. Now he is more inclined, though — along with his Indian friend, confidant and secretary Rabindra Nath Mitra — to skip over the religion and tell how his boyhood ambition was fired by glimpses of climbing parties and by older Sherpas' tales of them and the world. There seems room for both motives in his saga; but the change is there, and it reflects a general de-emphasis of the Buddhist faith in his affairs since last year. Even the Sherpa Buddhist Association — the Darjeeling Sherpas' mutual-aid society, of which Tenzing is now president — is dropping the word Buddhist from its name. One reason for this, it seems, is a touchiness here about religion, or superstition; Westerners scoff at it, so Easterners keep silent; Tenzing might be swayed that way by any Eastern friend who knew the West. Another reason, apparently, is the dread of communalism. India is threatened by divisiveness, in which religion plays a part. The Muslims broke off into Pakistan, some Sikhs wish to break off into their own Punjab, and so forth. Certain of the Hindus — India's leading majority — fear that Himalayan Buddhists may get the same idea. Tenzing respects feelings like that.

Ambitious or devout, Tenzing yearned for Darjeeling as he grew up. His father told him to stay home and herd yaks. He obeyed for a while, but at nineteen — in 1933 — ran away with some other young Sherpas. He came here, settled in Tung Soong Bustee, and did odd jobs like renting out the pony. Then in 1935 he was hired as a green porter for a British Everest party. He went again in '36 and '38, learning the things Sherpa guides must learn, including how to cook Western meals for Sahibs — his cooking is said to be good. The war suspended climbing for a decade, and since it resumed he has gone to Everest twice with the Swiss, in '52, and once with the British, in '53. In his career he has been to many other peaks as well. He has been through the mill. At times, one hears, he has been very down and very out, but long before his final success he was known as a top Sherpa sidar of this generation.

Another top sirdar is Ang Tharkay, who went with the French to Annapurna. Tenzing and Ang Tharkay began about the same time, and comparisons between them are made here. An Indian reporter in Darjeeling has put it this way: "Tenzing is debonair and smiling, Tharkay quiet and sure. Tenzing has the unquenchable fire of adventure in his eyes. Tharkay's gaze reflects a solid dependability like Everest. Tenzing's disarming chatter has the piquancy of spiced humor; Tharkay's few comments are seasoned with a wisdom as old as the mountains he climbs." Of Tenzing alone the same man says: "People call him 'Tiger of the Snows,' but I would call him the

'Laughing Cavalier.' " Tenzing's blithe spirit has regis-
tered with many. Karma Paul, a Darjeeling Tibetan who
managed expeditions in the thirties, when they passed
through his country — and who was an early employer of
Tenzing — says his smile and cheerfulness stood out from
the beginning. His modesty, too, is usually mentioned —
James Morris, the London *Times* man who went with
Hunt's party, speaks of it especially. And as he worked
up to sirdar Tenzing developed a gift of leadership. Ralph
Izzard of the *Daily Mail*, who was also with Hunt, writes
of Tenzing's "giving terse orders in a tone which commands instant obedience"; and says he had "all the bearing of a regimental sergeant major" when that was
needed. As one reads or hears about Tenzing on these
trips one concludes that he simply had what it took at
any given time — except, that is, for knowledge of things
like oxygen equipment. "He was astonishingly excellent
in courage and determination," Hunt has said, "and
physically wonderful." Mrs. Tenzing has spoken of his
passion for mountaineering.

Brought up near Everest, he had been on more Everest
parties than any other man, and he probably "deserved"
to climb it if anyone did. A Buddhist might argue that he
had been incarnated for that end. There have been striking turns of fate in the histories of Tenzing and of Everest climbing: the way Nepal opened up as Tibet closed,
for instance. Ang Tharkay might well have had Tenzing's place in '53, but he is an old associate of Eric Shipton, perhaps the leading British Himalayan climber, and

stays away from Everest unless Shipton is there too; he left the field to Tenzing in '53 and on both Swiss assaults of '52. Again, in '53 Tenzing and Hillary were not the first pair to try for the summit; two British climbers, Tom Bourdillon and Charles Evans, went ahead of them, but were stopped by oxygen failure. Yet again, the weather was perfect for Tenzing and Hillary, though the odds were against this. It seems as if barriers opened up when Tenzing drew near. The strain of the Swiss climbs in '52, plus a siege of malaria, had put him in bad shape at the start of '53, and this aroused comment when he joined Hunt at Katmandu in March. It might have kept him from the final assault, but between Katmandu and Everest he walked himself back into shape. This could be called psychosomatics rather than fate, of course, and it leads to the question of Tenzing's real attitude toward Everest climbing. Some here, including at least one sympathetic Westerner, maintain that he lacked a true mountaineer's interest in climbing, but went in '53, despite his bad health, to get money for his daughters' schooling. Others disagree and say Tenzing has long been set on climbing Everest, and has done special exercises in the off seasons to perfect himself for it. I have been told of a dinner given here in January of '53 — at Pliva's restaurant, a natural spot for banquets — where Tenzing vowed he would climb Everest or die. Before leaving to join Hunt he asked certain friends and acquaintances here, including Rabindra Nath Mitra and the deputy commissioner — Darjeeling's top official — to care for his family in the latter case. The gathering at Pliva's, I am also told, sent word to Colonel Hunt, through the Himalayan Club, asking that Tenzing be made a climber instead of merely a sirdar of Sherpa porters. There was pressure to this end in Nepal too, it is said — while the party was assembling — and the Swiss had set a precedent for it. The Swiss have no colonies and are unschooled in the British discipline about them. They treated Tenzing like a pal, as one man here puts it — and like a mountaineer in their own class. Tenzing and Raymond Lambert, a huge Alpine guide in the party, made the big try of the Swiss spring assault, and nearly got to the top. This was in the background when Hunt asked Tenzing at Katmandu to be one of the climbers — which was a bit like commissioning him from the ranks — though it is not set forth in Hunt's book. Hunt's book gives no sign that his motives were political. He seems a practical man throughout it — a man of discipline and action — whose will was bent entirely on getting a spearhead to the summit.

Whatever was thought and done then — or in the later weeks, when the party was secluded — Tenzing and Hillary reached the top on May 29. It was the end of the climb and the beginning of arguments. Argument number one was whether Tenzing or Hillary had got there first. This began in the outside world, amid a public conditioned to horse races and similar contests, where there must be a winner. Mountaineers seem to lack the winner feeling, especially when roped together. They progress as a unit, and apparently Hillary and Tenzing looked on themselves as that. When they descended they were drawn into the argument briefly, but got out again and said they had reached the top together, and this is their story now. The bad moment in that controversy, and others, came when the party rejoined the world at Katmandu. People there objected to news that Hunt and Hillary would be knighted while Tenzing would only be given the George Medal, a lower honor. (Even some British voices, including the Manchester *Guardian*'s, were raised against this.) Nepalese nationalism had been roused by Tenzing's feat, and Hunt made things worse by calling him a good climber "within the limits of his experience." It was a defensible remark, for Tenzing knows little, say, of rock climbing as practiced in Europe; but it sounded odd because he has more experience of Everest than any other human. Tenzing objected publicly, and became estranged from Hunt and the British. Feeling in Katmandu blazed higher. One hears in Darjeeling it was fanned by Nepalese Communists who hoped mob violence would be done to the British climbers, but this was averted and the party went to India, where its breach was patched up.

(There has been no public objection to the climb, incidentally, from Communists on the Tibetan, or Chinese, side. Tibet's border crosses Everest's summit, and one might expect the Reds to accuse Tenzing and Hillary of trespass when they stood there. Tenzing raised the flags of Britain, Nepal, India and the United Nations then, in a spot that looked down on Tibetan soil. There seems material for propaganda in this, but none has appeared. Nor has there been much attempt to claim Tenzing as a Tibetan, though one hears of gossip on this point in the Lhasa aristocracy. After the climb Tenzing was invited to a World Festival of Youth and Students at Bucharest, but he didn't go.)

The arguments subsided with time, and there is a wish to let them lie now, though people know they are there and step round them, sometimes awkwardly. One cliché about the West and the East is that the former stresses the individual and the latter the group. The Tenzing affair broke that rule. Hunt's expedition was a group undertaking in the supposed Oriental style, with each member humbly playing his part. Tenzing, on the other hand, could not be held in its framework, but popped out like a Westerner. Glory came to him that might have gone to the party as a whole. One can object and say that any of Hunt's climbers could have done what he did. But heroism seems to be subjective nowadays, not objective; a hero is a man who catches the public eye, not one who meets an abstract standard. Besides, if there *is* a standard in this case it can only be the climbing of Everest itself, whatever that is worth. It seems basically that men have tried to climb Everest to show their virility, a thing we Anglo-Saxons are much concerned with. Other motives have been given, but when these are pondered one concludes that they could be satisfied by any good climb short of the top. The try at ascent was long a test, promoted largely by men who believed in white superiority. In the end Tenzing, a nonwhite, passed it. Inevitably this has been seized on by Asian nationalists. Indians have technically got rid of Western rule, but in many respects are still awed by Western faces and ways. Tenzing is a Cinderella who shows them they too can be belles. This conflict is implicit in his case, and it seems useless to pretend otherwise.

Tenzing soars above the conflict as a rule, though he is sensitive and admits to feeling it when Westerners enter his museum and tell each other that many another Sherpa could have climbed Everest if properly led. He points to his chest and mutters about "something black inside" when describing such incidents; but he mentions them only when provoked, and in an emotional atmosphere; he seems happier when the mood is quiet and friendly. "Mountaineering must be friends," he says. "You help to me. I help to you. All same." He gets these word strings out slowly, thinking hard and making agonized if graceful gestures with his hands. "I say I first Hillary second. Hillary say Hillary first I second. No good. We both together." At the end of a speech like that he is apt to laugh and rest. To go much farther he needs an interpreter, and this is one way Rabindra Nath Mitra helps him. Mitra is a slight young Indian who grew up in Darjeeling and has a small printing shop here. He says he has taken an interest in Tenzing since 1950, when he was struck by his personality and tried, unsuccessfully, to arrange a lecture by him. In 1952 he began to publicize him in earnest, writing stories for the Indian press. One of these advanced the legend that Tenzing has three lungs, which caused Mitra to be criticized by Himalayan Club circles for money-making sensationalism. But he persisted. He encouraged Tenzing's ambition to climb Everest, and it was he who gave him the Indian flag to take there in 1953 — the expedition had planned on only the British, Nepalese and UN ones. After coming down from Everest Tenzing experimented with other secretaries, or advisers, but wasn't satisfied. Now he has apparently settled on Mitra for good. It is a trying job, for whoever holds it controls Tenzing to a large degree, and controls access to him, and thereby invites charges of favoritism. Mitra is a warm, idealistic young man who seems devoted to Tenzing, and it is believed he subordinates himself to the latter's interests as much as he can. But he sees them through the eyes of an Indian patriot and a Bengali as well — Bengalis, who spring from the plains round Calcutta, are often called emotional, and Mitra may contribute a bit of this air to Tenzing's surroundings. His closeness to Tenzing is resented, inevitably, but Tenzing seems unmoved by that. "People say this Bengali no good; only Tenzing good," he remarks, and his smile flashes. He speaks of "my friend Mitra" and seems to place utter confidence in him. Mitra too seems unmoved, relatively, by the jealousy. The other day he spoke of catching some newsreel men who were pretending to be amateurs and were shooting Mrs. Tenzing with gain in mind, which is not allowed. "I stopped them," he said, "and they complained, 'Oh, there is that Bengali chap.' " He shrugged when telling the story, but frowned too.

Mitra spends the day at Tenzing's flat, where he has a small office, behind the exhibit room — Tenzing is buying a house and will move soon, but the general layout cannot change much. The exhibit room is large and light, with windows looking toward the snows, over a veranda. The wall facing them holds the main display. It might be called a shrine. There is a picture of Gandhi at the top center, with Nehru below at one side and Queen Elizabeth and the Duke of Edinburgh at the other. Lower down is a framed Christmas card from the Duke, and still lower is one from Hunt addressed to "Tenzing of Everest." All round these, on the wall, are pictures of Tenzing at receptions, of his trip to England, and so forth. One large frame holds photos of a stay in Switzerland on the way home, where he posed in great bonhomie with his Swiss friends amid Alpine scenes — with Lambert on the Jungfrau, for instance.

A long table stretches across the wall below the pictures, and on it are souvenirs — plaques, medals, mugs; silver relief maps of the Himalayas, done with much artistic license. Below the table is a shelf where climbing boots are ranged; there are ten pairs of boots in the room altogether. On the wall to the right of the main exhibit is a smaller one devoted to the climb itself, crowned by a shot of Tenzing on the summit, this supported by more photos and more gear, such as the nylon rope that he and

Hillary used. Dozens of other things are placed here and there in the room — knives, clothes, ice axes, primus stoves, and so forth.

It is a pleasant room. The chairs have small Tibetan rugs on them, and often a tan-and-white fluffy Tibetan terrier as well, named Kangar — Tenzing got him on a trip to Lhasa with Professor Giuseppe Tucci, a noted Italian scholar. Kangar has three puppies on the premises. They are kept out of sight, but he is much in evidence himself, perhaps nuzzling someone, perhaps dashing out on the veranda to yap.

In this room Tenzing receives his callers, shows them his display and makes conversation with them. This isn't easy, for as a rule they have little real interest in his affairs. The other day I eavesdropped on a caller who spoke proudly of having read Hunt's book, and then asked what had become of the man who climbed Everest with Tenzing. "Oh, Hillary?" Tenzing said when he caught on. "Why, he is in New Zealand, I think." Then there was a pause. The caller offered Tenzing a cigarette, but he refused, saying he never smoked. The caller started to light one himself, then stopped and asked if it was all right. "O-o-o-o-oh, certainly," said Tenzing, all eagerness to get him an ash tray. Another pause. The caller looked out the window. The weather was clear, and he could see the distant snows. He remarked on how splendid they were, and Tenzing agreed. "Because one weeks ago weather always not so good," Tenzing said gropingly, "but today quite good." The caller asked if it would be clear right along now, with spring coming on. Tenzing allowed it would. "But Darjeeling also always September, October, November is the best season," he added, and smiled his dazzling smile and laughed his nervous laugh.

Such is his fate now, and it is doubtful if he likes it much. Some think Mrs. Tenzing likes it better. She seems less high-strung than he. In life she looks as she does in photographs: short, strong and capable. She has spent years in hard toil, carrying freight like firewood; she is not ashamed of this, and can still lift a huge load. She seems glad to pose for visitors' cameras, and she certainly likes the idea of money coming in. She has expanded her collection of the treasures Sherpa women go in for, which usually center round a Buddhist shrine in the main room of the house. In Tenzing's place the shrine is in back, where visitors seldom penetrate. It is smaller than the front room devoted to his public life, but is cozy, with Tibetan rugs, paintings and images, and shelves of brassware and crockery, including a set of fine Chinese teacups for which Mrs. Tenzing has had silver Tibetan lids and saucers made by local artisans. She runs a big household, for Tenzing is generous, and an Asian who does well usually attracts relatives. He feeds twenty mouths in the slack season now, Mitra says. One of his dependents is a retired Sherpa guide, older than he, a strong-featured man, straight as a ramrod, who acts as doorman and guard for the exhibit. Tenzing's teen-age daughters, Nima and Pempem, are not at home now, but are boarding at a Catholic convent here. The other day they emerged briefly when the American ambassador, George Allen, visited Darjeeling to give their father the Hubbard Medal of the National Geographic Society. On that occasion they wore blue serge dresses, white collars, white tam-o'-shanters and white bows in their dark braids. Every inch they were comely Asian girls being reared in respectability, with a Western touch.

The medal was presented in the Capitol Theatre, Darjeeling's main hall, before two hundred and fifty invited guests of all complexions and faiths. Tenzing wore a red turtle-neck sweater, gray plus fours, plaid stockings and brown shoes, and looked extremely handsome as he sat quietly in his chair on the stage. The day's first applause came when Mr. Allen referred to "Darjeeling, where you produce the greatest mountaineers in the world." The audience liked the idea. Yet Darjeeling's place as a mountaineers' home is shaky in truth, for it doesn't so much produce them as act as broker for them. A plan is now under way to remedy this by the founding here of a government mountaineering school, with Tenzing at its head. This scheme is ambitious and difficult, and it looms large in Tenzing's present affairs, which can be called a tangle. Tenzing differs from the Lindbergh style of hero in being accessible, and he differs from the Jack Dempsey style in having no head for business. Then there is his weakness with English, a tongue nearly indispensable for public heroism in the non-Communist world now. It is hard for us to imagine the handicap this makes for Tenzing, as even the most unlettered American would escape it. It goes with his innocence of legal usage. Tenzing is an intelligent man and has been much helped by Mitra and other friends, but it is doubtful if he knows where he stands in a business way. The main document governing him, before the school began to shape up, was a contract with the United Press, which he signed last year after going to England. It is understood to call for an autobiography, on which he and Mitra are now working and which James Ramsey Ullman, the mountaineering writer, is expected to take in hand later.* The contract, Tenzing and Mitra say, restricts his other activities till the book is published, but they seem at times to over-interpret it. A while ago Tenzing was invited, with expenses paid, to a fiftieth-anniversary dinner at the Explorers' Club in New York. He refused on the grounds that it might conflict with the U.P. contract. "Where I go people might take pictures of me," he explained at the time, "and write down what I say, and United States . . ." he fumbled, "and U.P. might not like it." He had only a vague idea of the U.P., it seemed, but was bent on treating it honorably. He has doubtless limited himself this way at other times. He does not object to the U.P. bonds, whether real or imaginary. He says the U.P.

* The book was published in 1955, under the title of *Tiger of the Snows.*

has helped him, and he is thankful and wants to be considerate. Before signing the contract he did a testimonial for Brylcreem, a hair unguent, but since then has turned all offers down. Mitra says he has had three or four from the movies, including one from Raj Kapoor, a gifted Indian producer. There is talk of getting the book out by October, and after that Tenzing will be in the public domain again and can try movies or anything else. He will also be more vulnerable. Mitra tells of people who invite him to functions, promising to pay expenses, and then fall through; or who try to get his name on testimonials by trickery. The U.P. contract helps fend these sharpers off, and Tenzing may feel exposed without it.

After Tenzing climbed Everest two purses were gotten up for him, each to buy a house. One was a public subscription in Nepal, which raised thirty thousand rupees, but did not spend them, as a Nepalese house was envisaged and Tenzing meanwhile returned to Darjeeling. At this writing ten thousand rupees have been sent from Nepal, and the remainder is in suspense. (A rupee is worth twenty-one American cents.) The other purse was raised by the *Statesman*, a Calcutta paper, and Tenzing's share was limited to twelve thousand rupees, anything over that being promised to the Himalayan Club for the use of Sherpas generally. There have also been individual gifts to Tenzing, as well as fees, and Mitra says he has received a total of sixty thousand rupees so far, of which he had spent fifteen thousand before buying the new house. The house is costing nearly forty thousand, including repairs. It can be assumed that Tenzing now owns it — less whatever mortgage it bears — plus his chattels and the equivalent of a few thousand American dollars. His post as head of the school carries eight hundred and fifty rupees a month, and he holds a trucking license that brings in several hundred more. This is a government perquisite too, special to the region. The roads round Darjeeling are so narrow, steep and twisting that the number of vehicles allowed on them is strictly limited. Permits for these are sure money-makers and are sometimes given to worthy citizens who need extra income. Tenzing has one — as has Ang Tharkay — and officials here say it should bring five hundred to one thousand rupees clear profit a month if handled right. So besides his capital, and any contracts with the outside world, Tenzing has an income here equal to a few hundred dollars monthly.

By Sherpa standards this is vast wealth. A common Sherpa porter gets three rupees a day, plus food, while working. A sirdar gets five to ten rupees, plus food. By going twice with the Swiss in 1952 — which apparently taxed him to the limit — Tenzing made eighteen hundred rupees, or something under four hundred dollars, which must have been close to the Sherpa record for a year's take. Now he makes ten, twenty or thirty times that, and has thus both drawn away from other Sherpas and incurred an obligation to help them. Sherpa climbers past their prime have an especially hard lot, for they have rarely saved money. The most famous Sherpa of the twenties and early thirties, Lakpa Chedi, was taken to England and France, feted there, and praised by Sir Francis Younghusband, who said his name should be written in letters of gold along with Mallory's. Now he is a doorman standing outside a Calcutta store, dim-looking if erect. Yet he has fared better than many other old Sherpas, who are derelicts here or burdens on their families. Tenzing himself, now in his forties, is nearing the age when Sherpas must slacken off, and that he can do so in such unprecedented circumstances is resented inevitably. The pony I saw him riding near Tung Soong Bustee had cost eight hundred rupees, I learned later, and this was more than most Sherpas in the neighborhood have ever owned. A Sherpa can't live in Darjeeling like an ordinary man of the world without going high-hat by Sherpa standards.

Tenzing's wish to help other Sherpas seems heartfelt. Besides feeding the extra mouths at home he does numerous things for Sherpas on the outside, individually and as a group. Recently a Calcutta music firm recorded a song in praise of Tenzing and offered him royalties, but he had them turned over to the Sherpa Association. Then there is the collection box, at his exhibit, for the Sherpa Climbers' Benevolent Fund. (The association is for all Sherpas in Darjeeling, and the fund for climbers alone; they have special need because of the risks they run.) Through the association Tenzing is trying also to furnish Sherpas to expeditions, in rivalry with the Himalayan Club and with a view to raising wages. But it seems doubtful if the club will be supplanted easily. Club rates may be low, but they are in keeping with the law of supply and demand — or the law of supply anyway: lots of Sherpas, here and in Namche Bazar, are glad to work for them. Tenzing may be about to learn one of the bitterest lessons of postwar Asia — that organizing Eastern products for the Western market is harder than it looks. Western buyers must be persuaded that they will get exactly what they order. The British in Asia have excelled at this job, and have cast a sort of sterling hallmark on the things they have handled, whether teak, bristles or mountain porterage. Asians have not done well, in the past decade, at taking the business over from them. They don't inspire the same confidence. The Himalayan Club enjoys the British name for reliability, which is especially important in its field. It seems doubtful whether groups in distant lands, planning complex trips on tight schedules, will desert the old firm for Tenzing, however much they sympathize with him. This is another condition of the Sherpas' rockbound life.

The school project shares Tenzing's desire for a new Sherpa deal, but goes farther; it seeks to harness him in the cause of Indian nationalism as a whole. Sherpas are Indian only in that they come to India for work. They are one of several Mongoloid hill peoples who differ from the Indians in viewpoint and have been politically separate from them during most of history. Yet if India

is to run well as a nation she must absorb these hill peoples, and she seeks to do so. It was suitable, therefore,
that Tenzing should become an Indian hero, and he fitted
into the role well — fitted in literally, indeed, for on
reaching New Delhi he found he could wear the clothes
of Pandit Nehru, India's senior hero, as if they had been
tailored for him. Nehru lent him a wardrobe suited for
state occasions, and he took this to London, where he
appeared in it with an air of smartness and Indianness
combined. Since then he and Nehru have had a warm
relationship based on much more than identical size. One
Indian here says Nehru has been so much hero-worshiped
that he welcomes the chance to hero-worship someone
else. Another says he is an enthusiast of the outdoors who
respects Tenzing as a master in that field. Many, of
course, say the two men respond to elements of greatness
in each other. Anyway, they are close. Tenzing stays
with Nehru when he visits New Delhi, and there is said
to be almost a father-and-son feeling between them.
Other Indian statesmen have taken Tenzing up too, including Dr. B. C. Roy, the Chief Minister of West Bengal, the state in which Darjeeling is located. Dr. Roy was
the first to suggest the school, when the Everest party
returned from Katmandu after the climb. They landed at
Calcutta and were received, and Dr. Roy asked if a school
in Darjeeling would be possible. Hunt, Hillary and Tenzing all said yes, and the school has been on paper since
then. Its title is the Himalayan Institute of Mountaineer-

ing and Research, and Tenzing's title is Chief Instructor.

It is still on paper after these months, despite close attention from the Darjeeling authorities. It is a novel venture for India, and a substantial one — its cost is figured at two million rupees in the end. The documents on it must be approved by government financial people and by experts, and they move slowly from bureau to bureau. So far Tenzing has been appointed, a permanent site for the school has been chosen here, and a temporary home for it has nearly been rented — a big stucco villa a few miles from town. It is on a steep slope and looks over a valley in the Darjeeling style, but there are no peaks or snows near by, and this seems to be the school's main drawback. For all its history as a mountaineers' base Darjeeling is not in real mountains itself. The nearest big-time ones are on the skirts of Kanchenjunga, a week distant by foot. The plan at this writing is to start each class here and then take it to the Kanchenjunga neighborhood by stages. So two weeks will be added to the time spent in high-altitude climbing, and non-Indian pupils may not care for that when other mountains are accessible round the globe. Then Kanchenjunga is near the touchy frontier of Red Tibet, and India has stopped nearly all travel by foreigners in that zone for the present. As for Indian pupils, it must be said that the school is backed more by their government than by their culture. Through history Indians have seen little need to climb the high Himalayas for sport, and it isn't sure they will see much now. These obstacles will be felt, it is expected, as the school moves off paper, but it is possible they will be taken in stride. Anything seems possible in the Himalayas.

So far the school's main achievement has been to institutionalize Tenzing as a national hero. After the United Press agreed to the recent Explorers' Club junket, for instance, the West Bengal Government forbade it, saying the school was in a formative stage and Tenzing couldn't be spared. Whether this was the government's real reason or not, the incident showed how it can sway Tenzing's affairs. Indian officials seem proud of Tenzing and keen to help him. The best help they can think of, perhaps, is to make him one of themselves: a member of India's idealistic leadership — the member in charge of mountaineering endeavor. Anyone who sees Tenzing fidget here while the school gestates must question the fitness of this; but it hardly matters, for Tenzing seems fated now to be a dream personality in large part. He has a strong nature of his own, but to most people he is what they make him — a Sherpa folk hero, a porter gone wrong, a jewel of the officialdom. These dream Tenzings are in their early stages, and they may develop farther, or others may open up. There is, for instance, the possibility of a commercialized dream Tenzing in the American style. Tenzing hopes to get his book out this October, and he may visit America then with India's blessing. He may well make a hit there, and one can imagine our streets thronged by junior Sherpas roped together and picking away with junior ice axes. Tenzing might start something like that, or he might go in other directions.

But wherever he is going he is still en route. Everest, it seems, was just a station.

NOTE: The Himalayan Institute was officially opened by Pandit Nehru in November, 1954, and has been giving special mountain training to Indian Army personnel. As for Tenzing's trip to America, he is still hoping to make it as this book goes to press, in 1956.

Nine Hundred Mules

ONE HEARS much now of the approaches to China, including the southwest one, from Burma. I have learned something about that route from my brother Jake, who traveled it late in the Japanese war, though using a kind of transport now thought obsolete — he rode in with nine hundred artillery mules that had fought in Burma and were destined for the Chinese Army. The trip was seven hundred and fifty miles long and took over two months; in this respect, I believe, it was on a scale with the old cavalry marches of the Civil War and the Indian wars, though of course there was no fighting. It may also have been the last big animal movement in U.S. military history, for one hears that the army mule is being replaced by helicopters — these are now expected to do all a mule can do, though Jake thinks that is absurd on its face; helicopters can't, for instance, walk silently down a road at night when fully loaded, he says. Anyway — last of their race or not — his mules went uncomplainingly into China, a land not wholly suited to them. They plodded through walled towns that Marco Polo had known and they rolled in old graveyards while stone dragons watched. They came through in good shape too, but when the trip was over disaster struck them and few lived to tell the tale, if that is what mules do.

In May of that year — 1945 — Jake had found himself in charge of thirteen hundred mules and horses pooled outside Myitkina, the chief American base in Upper Burma. Plain American mules made up ninety-eight per cent of this herd, the rest being American, Australian and Indian horses the Army had picked up by trade, theft and purchase along the line. Most of the animals came from the pack artillery, as Jake did himself — he was a captain, thirty years old — and had been fighting the Japanese in the Central Burma campaign just finished. At Myitkina Jake and the handful of artillerymen with him were in suspense. They believed — rightly, it turned out — that the Japanese had left Burma altogether, and they were waiting to see where the mules might be wanted next. The strongest rumor had them passing the summer where they were, which didn't sound bad. The climate was good there, and the country was flat or gently rolling, like upstate New York. The outfit had masses of barbed wire, and they were fencing in a pasture about a mile square; they were also building some sheds, and of course riding herd a lot. In their spare time they had begun exploring the jungle, shooting doves and finding elephant wallows; they had good swimming and appeared to be set for a long, pleasant stay, a dream they were waked from by the sudden arrival of a colonel from China, a tall old pack artilleryman from the boots-and-breeches or campaign-hat times, not yet much mechanized. He flew in one day.

"We want these mules in China as soon as we can have them," he said. "How long would you need to get ready for the trip?"

"Ten days," Jake answered, "if we had our supplies at the outset." Then the colonel flew away.

China and Burma were different realms then in the U. S. Army as in world politics. One was in the China Theater and one in the India-Burma Theater, and they had few real links except at top levels. To Jake the China Theater was an unknown land, cut off by a vast emptiness. Now, after the colonel's departure, an impulse struggled back across this emptiness and Jake was ordered, through Burma channels, to march nine hundred mules into the Southwest China base of Kunming, starting in ten days. He was offered nine hundred men for the trip — a man a mule — but he asked for only three hundred, and in the end got but two hundred and forty, which was typical of his fate with supplies.

The expedition had special needs, the chief of them being "shoes, mule" in Army language — mules' feet are longer and narrower than those of horses, which wear shoes, horse. Two tons of shoes were needed to carry on the road, and one ton was needed to nail on in the ten days before starting, as lots of the mules had gone barefoot in pasture. Jake asked for a generator so they could do the shoeing on a round-the-clock basis, and he got not one, but four in succession, and each broke down.

Artillery mules wear packsaddles — as Jake has explained to me — with heavy steel frames on quilted wool stuffed with hair. It takes two men to lift one of these saddles by itself, without a load, and they bear down hard and give mules sore backs unless carefully fitted. So every pack outfit has a crew of saddlers and pack masters, with canvas bags of extra hair, and needles and hooks for putting it in and taking it out of the stuffing, and small thongs for quilting the wool; each night these men — in theory at least — remake saddles that have rubbed. Jake looked for a bad time with his mules' backs, which were soft from two months of no packing. He had suggested that most of the saddles be forwarded by truck, together with all the supplies possible, while the mules were herded loose. But the colonel from China had vetoed this, perhaps from romantic old-style notions. At least the party had good saddlers and pack masters. At the outset it was determined that the mules should be split into three sections, or "serials," of three hundred each, which would travel a day apart, for less strain on grazing spots, water holes and ferries. The specialists were divided between these serials, and supplies were ordered to match: three saddler's chests; eighteen pack master's rolls; six buzzy cots, or pack kitchens; six forges; and six sets of blacksmith's tools. Among the more general items asked for were six hundred mantas, or canvas sheets to cover loads; five hundred halters; eight hundred halter shanks; and two thousand lash ropes — not to mention all the human gear needed to put two hundred and forty men on the road. Some of these things reached the party before it left. Some didn't. Some reached the Myitkina supply depot in time, but in carefree style were given to other mule outfits summering near by.

A few men joined the party by volunteering, as if it were a force being raised outside the Army system. The party had no doctors assigned to it, though it was plain that one would be needed — with a couple of medic GIs — in each serial. Luckily there was a medical unit in Myitkina at the time, headed by a Captain Bennett, a graduate of Dartmouth and Camp Hale, the Army ski school — a short, thick, genial man inured to the Army, the theater, and the confusion of both. He was bored with Myitkina and thought the trip sounded interesting, so he fell in with it and persuaded many in his unit to join him. They came freely and were free to leave. Five weeks out on the road one of them simply took off — he thought his transfer home might be coming, and he wanted to be where he could receive it. Jake could do nothing about this: he had no orders to hold him.

Two days of grace were added to the original ten for preparation, which didn't make much difference; and half shod, with packsaddles half fitted — half baked in every way — the first serial took to the road before dawn of May 26, in blackness and drenching rain. Jake and his men opened the gate and herded the mules out vaguely, and had little idea of what was going. That day the first serial crossed the Irrawaddy. The mules went a few dozen at a time in a little GI ferry, driven by outboard-motor boats, which was swept far downstream on each crossing — they looked uncomfortable jammed behind the ferry's railings, but they took it calmly, as mules take most things.

The first serial camped on the east bank that night, the second crossed the next day, and the third crossed two days later, having lingered to shoe some mules and clean up. After the river they all had three days' marching on the flat, where they could shake down a bit, and then they started into the hills toward the border. These were the beginning of the Hump, the great hurdle that our American supplies to China had to cross during the war — by plane alone for most of it. Now the land routes, such as they were, had been opened. The famous Burma Road lay some distance to the south at this point, and the party was embarking on a short cut that would meet it later on, in China — the Myitkina-Lungling Cutoff, better known as the Cheeves Highway, for an SOS general who had put it through. It turned out to be a jerry-built affair and was washing away — despite some U.S. engineers and hordes of Chinese coolies posted on it — in the rains then beginning. Jake's men got a jeep over it, but soon after that it fell apart for good. They possessed three trucks also, on which they had put the blacksmiths, and their equipment; but these went round by the Burma Road to wait up ahead at a rendezvous.

The cutoff was a muddy red gash through green forest, and the party sloshed up it, back and forth over hairpins, always up. The green was the bright green of New England in June, Jake says, and it had a sweet smell, though less sweet than that of the true lowland jungles; it was a mass of trees, vines, creepers, bamboos and ferns, and monkeys chattered in it. The men were bothered in their climb by flies and mosquitoes, but the mules with their tough skins didn't seem to mind these. The mules put up with the rain and the tedious going; they had been simple beasts of burden — no more, no less — for a long time, and they seemed to accept that fate wholly. Nine tenths of them went on without incident, though the others gave some trouble. They were being led, hitched one before another in strings of four or five each, and often a mule would stop quickly for a washout or some tempting grass, and his rotten old lead rope would part. Then he would be left to go loose for the rest of that day, to save time, though Jake admits this is not the way to handle loaded animals on unfamiliar roads.

There were moments of clearness and hot sun, but then a downpour would blur things out. It made Jake think of *The Rains Came* by Louis Bromfield, which he had read a few years before. The men's clothes and the packs got wet, and so did the leather and the saddle linings, and they rubbed the mules and made them sore; at night in the rain the mules stood with their backs up and their hindquarters to the wind; they slipped about in the mud; the grain got wet when it was fed to them; and the halter ropes shrank and were hard to untie. Rain messes up an outdoor unit like that; if you have trucks you can get into them, but they had only bits of canvas — jungle hammocks and ponchos — inadequately supplied at Myitkina. Often the cooks couldn't light their fires, and the goal of all was to dry out occasionally, not to keep from getting wet.

The party was looking forward to the Chinese border and also to a place called Sadon Pa, a few days short of it in Burma. After the border, they had been vaguely told, "China" would take care of them. They didn't know what "China" meant in this phrase — the China Theater, they generally assumed. But at least it would be a change, for better or worse, and they looked toward it with interest. Their prospect at Sadon Pa was more concrete: a stockpile of rations for man and beast was waiting there. But when they reached it they found the pile had been badly covered with a little canvas and was mainly spoiled. There were six hundred bags — thirty tons — of grain, but they found they could use or carry away only three hundred and fifty of them, and in these most of the contents were wet and some were moldy.

The border, which they crossed on June 2, a week out of Myitkina, was in a saddle, on the backbone of the Hump, 12,260 feet high. A sign was planted there saying

BURMA and CHINA in English, and above it stood a festive, if rickety, bamboo arch draped in evergreens. Behind the men lay Burma and the jungle they had known so intimately. Ahead was something quite different: a huge, open, seemingly barren landscape. There were no woods or trees in sight there, and the view seemed to stretch away forever, into the China Theater with its unknown ways. The weather too was clearer and more open, and there was a psychological change: a wondering, curious, hopeful pause. Since Jake had been in the Army one strange step had led to another — Australia, Bombay, Calcutta, a midnight flight to Myitkina for action against the Japanese — each step a farther one from home and things familiar — and at times he had stopped and wondered about these places and how he had got to them. This was such a time.

From the border they dropped down to their first big Chinese valley, and in three days they came on the plain to the walled city of Tengchung, which had good water and grass, and where their trucks with the blacksmiths were waiting, having come north from the Burma Road on a Chinese highway. They lay up there nearly a week. Many of the mules had sore backs, and all were hungry; their bellies were drawn up and they had been snatching at every green thing on the road. Now they fed steadily. There was baled hay at Tengchung, and when tied on the picket line they ate this; when turned loose they grazed feverishly; and after three or four days they were filled to normal again. Meanwhile the men rested and washed their clothes; they found some army engineers in Tengchung and worked trades with them for odds and ends.

The engineers had a radio and airstrip, and Jake started at once to importune Kunming, the capital of his new world. He wanted to get some trucks and stop using the packsaddles; he says he knew that the mules and the saddles could both be delivered in better shape that way. He wanted water-heating equipment, as the men's drinking water had to be boiled against dysentery, and wood had grown scarce when they entered China. And he wanted funds to buy vegetables for brightening their ten-in-one rations. He sent a radio message asking for these things or for orders to fly into Kunming to requisition them, and the next day a pilot came in a liaison plane to fetch him.

He had had dreams of what Kunming — the Army side — would be like, but none matched the reality in splendor, he says. The European war was past by then, and great organisms, it seemed, were building up to end the Asiatic war with dignity. Besides the SOS, there was a Chinese Combat Command in Kunming, a Chinese Training Command and a Rear Echelon, not to mention the Fourteenth Air Force and the ATC. Soon after landing, Jake found himself being ushered into huge offices filled with desks, at each of which sat a colonel or lieutenant colonel. He was shuffled back and forth between them, bewildered. He had really not known there were

so many colonels in the whole Army, let alone Kunming.
He had thought that if a captain, like himself, got into a
full colonel's office, he did a lot of saluting and clicking
of heels; but here the colonels were like so many cor-
porals or T5s. One colonel wrote out a memo and gave
it to a clerk, saying, "Take this captain over to Colonel
So-and-so and tell him to fix him up." The clerk took
him. "What is it you're doing out there, Rand?" the second colonel asked. Jake told him. "You mean you're
walking out there with all those mules?" The colonel
looked as if he couldn't believe it, but Jake told him it
was true. "Then it's trucks you want?" the colonel said.
"Of course we'll fix you up. How many trucks?" Jake
stayed in Kunming three days and got everything he was
after: three British lorries, a musette bag of money — one
million Chinese dollars — and permission to turn the saddles in. Then he flew back to the life he had known and
rejoined the mule column, which was under way again.

They were on the Burma Road now, settled down for
steady going, their mules packless and herded free. That
part of the road crosses a series of valleys, at right angles
— the greatest are those of the Salween and Mekong
Rivers — and the march had a wavy rhythm, a rise and
fall each few days. The high ground they passed was
brown, treeless, in brush and weeds. The low ground had
opened into picture-book Chinese landscapes, following
the promise of the border — mirrorlike rice paddies step-
ping down terrace by terrace, some with pale-green seed-

lings in the water, some being plowed by slow gray buffaloes, leg deep in the mud. Now and then a loose buffalo
took up with the mules and followed them awhile, though
the men didn't load any with packsaddles, a stunt they
had once tried in Burma. They rode slowly on in the dry
June sun.

Nearly always at midafternoon they reached some
grass and stopped; usually Jake had found it beforehand
by jeep reconnaissance, and usually it was in a graveyard; in that part of China the other good land was taken,
to the last inch, by rice and vegetables. The grass in the
night's cemetery would already have been grazed by
native animals, some of which might be around, and
often the mules would chase them, ganging up with
clique psychology on strangers; in one graveyard they
nearly ran down and killed a mare and foal. Once in
possession they would start rolling. Mules like grass to
roll on, Jake says, though he thinks they prefer sand or
gravel; in Burma he had once been able to drive some
mules onto a gravel island in a stream, where they could
take turns rolling and standing their tired legs in the
water, and this had plainly been heaven to them; they
roll for the scratching, according to Jake — they are
most apt to do it when packs are taken off. Now, after
rolling, these mules would graze till suppertime, while the
men sat and watched them like cowherds, a job for which
they had a rotating crew drawn from all hands but the
cooks and blacksmiths; the latter rode the trucks and
arrived early at the camp sites, where they would set up

their stoves and forges and get ready; they were busiest when the main body was resting. Before supper five or six other men would string up the picket line — a good length of inch or three-quarter-inch rope, anchored to trees if some could be found, or to posts or trucks if not; the men would strain over the job, making the rope taut with a sheepshank — a big crew of them heaving in muscular ceremony. Most of the graveyards had old tombs with swooping roofs and stone monsters, and weeds and bushes grew from them till they seemed part of the land; bones and skulls often lay round; and the men would run their jungle hammocks from the tombs and might use the skulls to decorate these for the night. Such affairs would take them till dark, when they would tie the mules to the picket line and turn in. Next day they would break camp quickly and be on the road again.

The party couldn't have proper morning reports or count the men as one should in the Army — they herded themselves as they did the mules. Jake never really knew their strength, for if a man took sick he was apt to fall out quietly, perhaps hitching a truck ride to Kunming. About ninety men fell out when they reached the first GI field hospital on the road, and some never came back. The unit was not regular. Most of the men wore fatigues, but some had big Australian hats from Burma, and others picked up straw Chinese coolie hats on the way. The route-order or Wild West spirit was strongest in the second serial, which had more than its share of former cowboys and mule skinners; their dress was the most fantastic of all, and they spent the most time shooting crows, with carbines or forty-fives, and eating them too if their bragging could be believed. The first serial was led by a chief warrant officer, John Blackburn of Roaring River, North Carolina, a pack-artillery expert, an old hand who had been everywhere in the peacetime Army; who had been a *cargador*, horseshoer, pack master, stable sergeant and saddler at one time or another; who knew all there was to know about mules and loads. He broke trail for the rest. The third serial was a special job, as it had to pick up stragglers from the first two and solve other hang-over problems before the expedition disappeared from a scene forever. It was in the hands of Captain Bill Sausser, a self-reliant cowboy from the West, very rugged. Sausser loved horses, Jake says, and through trades was always getting one of his own, which he would bring into as close a relationship with himself as he could — not taking it into his tent, for there wasn't room, but tying it as near as possible. Before this phase of their life he and Jake had commanded pack batteries in the same battalion; Sausser had been Western in his style and Jake Eastern, but they had gotten on well, making allowances for each other. Before they left Myit-kina Sausser had asked Jake if he could take four or five mules and trade them for horses with some of the other mounted outfits near by, and in agreeing Jake had suggested he get a horse for him too. Sausser had brought Jake something to the Eastern, rather than Western, taste — a lightweight brown Australian mare, like a thoroughbred in type. "I thought she was your kind," he had said, "I thought you'd like her," and Jake did. She was quiet and sensible, with no bad habits, and popular with the mules of the first serial, with whom she spent her time.

Jake's own road time was spent half on the mare, riding with the first serial, and half in the jeep. The jeep stayed in the hands of a Staff Sergeant Cogdill of Balsam, North Carolina, a GI who Jake says was so able in every way — with mules, men, mountains and Army life in the field — that he logically became the unit's executive officer, though they had some lieutenants along. Every few days Jake would drive forward in the jeep with Cogdill and find camp sites for the next few nights — they were only sixteen miles apart on an average. If there was good reason Jake might jeep back to the second and third serial, though he did this rarely; or the third could send word forward, if need be, via an ambulance that traveled with it. The party's main contact, though, was in especially grassy places where they could lie over two or three days, with all the serials gathered in close together, grazing and shoeing. Jake used these times to talk things over with the serial commanders and to catch up on administration.

He says it was fun to compare his two speeds — in the jeep and in the saddle. In a day's jeeping he could easily cover five days' mule march, chopping along and bouncing on the rough road. Then he would come back and retrace the sortie, at a different pace, with time to see the

details of the landscape and ponder the strange country
he had grown part of. In the jeep the feeling was "Hurry
up and win the war." In the saddle it was "Take it easy,
the war will last a long time." The mules' pace prevailed
when one was with them.

Some called these nine hundred mules the most pre-
cious herd on record, as each stood for an outlay by the
U.S. of maybe three thousand dollars, in purchase, transport, training, feed and care. But they could also be
called worthless, as they had been classed expendable for
action in Burma, and through chance alone had not been
spent. Jake's own view was that they had worked their
way and owed the government nothing, despite their
cost. As for their nature, they were mules. All mules
have their own personalities, Jake says, but they fall into
types as soldiers do. Some of these were businesslike and
went to their work without thought of the others; they
stood still while being loaded or handled, and marched
quietly all day. Others were always out of line and cussed
— kicking and bucking — making it hard for the men.
And others kept bothering their fellow mules, putting
their ears back and nipping. Mules come from the union
of jackasses and mares (the animal called the hinny, which
comes from the reverse union, of stallions and she-asses,
is seldom found). They inherit many traits of horses,
according to Jake, but differ from them in having
tougher feet and hardier constitutions, in being surer
footed, and in tending to quit when exhausted, as some

horses do not, which can save them from being worked to death. Jake had been snobbish about mules when he joined the pack artillery, as had others who were used to horses, but he had long ago got over this in the tough Burma going. Mules are not built for speed, he says, as they have short vertical shoulders, but they can do prodigious things. He has seen them climb to places where he couldn't go without the full use of hands and feet. He has seen them drop into gorges and disappear far below, turning over and over, vague masses of feet and ears and load; and when he has gotten down there he has found them sometimes with neck or back broken, but often on their feet, quietly grazing. Their silence on the move is striking. Once on a night exercise in the Rockies, in training, Jake had had to move a battery an hour's march on a soft, sandy road; he had been at the head of the column, which included eighty mules, fully loaded, and except for a rare cough, or rattle of some metal part, he had been unable to tell they were behind him without looking back and seeing them in the moonlight.

The party was not without guides. An interpreter, Major Ping, had been assigned to it in Myitkina — a tiny Chinese, enthusiastic and helpful in spirit, though not fluent with English or familiar with this Burma frontier country — he had lived his life in the Westernized seaports of East China till the war had dislodged him. Glad as Jake was to have him, he had felt he could use supplementary talent. Before leaving Myitkina he had made a reconnaissance toward the border and en route had seen a number of Chinese pack trains — five, ten or twenty little mules or horses each, with their *ma-fu*, or grooms. He had asked Major Ping about the chances of getting some *ma-fu* to guide the expedition, and the latter had gone into Myitkina and enlisted three of them, one for each serial. Though the party had trouble communicating with these men, they helped it greatly by pointing out short cuts — safe, if rocky, paths across the bases of hairpins, for example. Their only fault was one of scale. Their own animals were not much bigger than burros or Shetland ponies and were led unshod by the *ma-fu* on foot — were far different from these big American mules, about eighty of which in each serial had riders. Trails that seemed good to a *ma-fu* and his ponies would seem cramped to the American mules as they tried slipping their big feet in between the boulders.

One morning the first serial crossed a pass and stood at the head of a valley that seemed three days' march in extent. It was a quiet place, and above it to the right a white temple stood against the brown hillside. Below it lay a village, and far off to the left the road slowly hairpinned down to this; it looked a full day's march, though onto the village itself the men could nearly throw a stone. But a small trail led down that way, seemingly as the crow flies, and Jake decided to take it on his *ma-fu*'s advice, though he knew it was a risk. It turned out to be of stone steps, very old; Marco Polo had traveled this route in the thirteenth century, and one could believe the steps had been there then; tracks had been worn in them, deep in the stone — short ones like ponies' hoofs and long ones like people's feet. After the party had gone down awhile it grew plain that the steps were wretchedly slippery for the mules, with their shoes, and small too, as a man would find stairs small in a midget's house. Yet they couldn't turn back safely, for the path was narrow and dropped away on the right side to a gorge, with boulders and rushing water and cascades. By now the men had all dismounted. Jake was in front, leading his mare, knowing he had made a mistake and sweating it out. He sent back word for the rear men to pick up all the shoes they found pulled off in the tricky going, and in the end they brought down sixty-six. There were no other casualties, through good luck, but Jake vowed he would never again put Western mules in such a place.

Major Ping's main duty was to help draw supplies from the Chinese SOS, which the China Theater had told to support the expedition. The SOS depots were usually in old temples, and they were supposed to furnish straw; horse beans, which were like thick dried limas; and occasionally salt, though it was like gold in that country — Jake saw goiters in every town there. It was a while before the mules came to like the beans, and the straw they never liked; yet the party always had trouble cajoling these supplies from the SOS; they never got enough of them, which was why they had to graze so much. Indeed the beans they fed their reluctant mules had great value for the Chinese in that region; not only did the SOS hate to part with them; but the men found they could trade them readily to the natives at their camp sites for vegetables, laundry service and other needs; and when they left in the mornings the people would go to their picket line and hunt there for beans the mules had ground into the earth. It was a poor part of China, made so by years of supporting the war, Jake gathered, and often he came on beggars nearly dead or corpses swarmed about by flies. There was a question whether the human standard of living there was up to that of the American mules; Chinese troops would be met on the road, with their packs and bags of rice and shoulder poles, and they would seem more thoughtlessly loaded than these mules had ever been. Then there was a question as to how much China could absorb of Western supplies. Crossing the Hump, the party had traveled along the new pipeline that was supposed to run gasoline into the country, and already it had been cut in many places, looted and left to leak away, keeping the GI pump-station crews always busy. They had come on German artillery pieces that were not in action but hoarded by some general against the future. The uses of these and other Western things had been transformed, it seemed, to their detriment. Jake and his men wondered how their mules might be used in the game, though the mules themselves didn't wonder, so far as they could see. The mules clacked noncommittally on the flagstones of the Chinese towns, in through the West Gate, out through the East Gate, sometimes poking their noses

into the shop fronts between. In the open they walked
silently and looked for grass. And day by day, slowly,
they drew nearer Kunming.

On July 16 the party reached Tsuyung, the last big
town before Kunming and one hundred and ninety kilos
short of it. Tsuyung had become a minor Army center.
With the growth of the road it had sprouted an ord-
nance truck-repair station, a fuel dump and a stockpile
of parts, and the road's long convoys always stopped
there. As a town it was about the size of Tengchung,
where the mules had got their first rest after the border,
but now the circumstances were different. The mules
were not thin, ravenous or sore of back; they moved like
Old China Hands onto the Tsuyung airstrip, and grazed
in a matter-of-fact way. The men had changed too: they
were road-hardened and did things automatically; and
they were well heeled, as for some time they had been
drawing B rations, PX supplies and fresh meat from the
Army apparatus on the road. They were in richer country logistically. There was a good telephone from Tsuyung to Kunming, and the Signal Corps was more active
in all ways; one could, in fact, drive to Kunming in a
day by jeep, which gave Tsuyung a plush feeling.

The first serial camped at Tsuyung for three days,
and in that time got the accounts squared. In spending
the million dollars he had drawn Jake was supposed, by
Army procedure, to get a voucher for everything he
bought — a bill stamped with the chop, or Chinese seal,

of the merchant. This had been impossible in much of the back country as they had bought vegetables from peasants there who had never seen chops. Now in Tsuyung they found merchants, already wise in Uncle Sam's bookkeeping, who would make up bills and chop them on request, if only they were given other business on the side. The first serial took advantage of this. Then it moved on and left Tsuyung to the second and third serials. The third never got farther, it turned out in the end.

The last stretch — the one hundred and ninety kilos — took the first serial ten days in easy stages. On the evening of the ninth they camped in a suburb three miles to Kunming's west — a new place with modernistic stucco houses; they had trouble finding a camp site there but at length came on a piece of grass and were allowed to use it after Jake had written out a statement, for the caretaker, of military necessity. The next day they entered the city by the West Gate, after more suburbs. The city wall, of brownish-gray stone, loomed high and solid, and Kunming itself was much bigger than the other towns they had gone through — not different essentially, but bigger in all things, including GI activity; jeeps darted everywhere. The men rode through the main street, smart on the asphalt, while hundreds — thousands — of Chinese gaped at the size of the mules and their turnout. Then they went a few miles east of town and reached their exact goal, Hostel 9, the Field Artillery Training Center, where American officers were coaching and equipping Chinese artillery. Jake turned over the first-serial mules to the FATC at once, though they were slow in passing from there to Chinese hands — floods in the east kept them from moving to front-line units. For this reason the second and third serials were held back on the road for the time being, the third at Tsuyung and the second at Kilo 51, where there was good grazing. Though Jake no longer controlled the first-serial mules he saw a lot of them around the training center, where he took up residence. They were picketed on the parade ground, and being reshod and undergoing veterinary "processing." A strange disease had appeared among them, weakening and killing the few mules it had attacked, but on the whole they looked well. The numerous colonels at the training center spoke glowingly of their appearance, and Jake was proud. On the road he had lost but twenty-seven of them — three per cent — which everyone agreed was a low figure in view of the problems.

Hostel 9 was a fine building put up by the Chinese to house Americans, and Jake moved in to enjoy novelties like showers, electric lights and tablecloths. It was fearfully comfortable. Many of his comrades from Burma were there, having come on to China for liaison work when the fighting was done, and he spent much time in reunions. His duties weren't heavy. He had equipment to turn in yet, but the men of the first serial, like the mules, had joined the FATC. The second and third serials, of which Jake was still in charge, were stationary now and able to take care of themselves. He often jeeped out to see them, perhaps to spend the night, and they were well fixed. Sausser had got hold of some pyramidal tents and pitched them on the Tsuyung airstrip. He had also got hold of a phonograph, some Western records and a red roan horse. The roan was hobbled, Western style, outside Sausser's tent, from which cowboy songs issued day and night — "Oh, That Strawberry Roan" being the usual choice.

But the ailment of the mules got worse. It had appeared in all three serials now and had been diagnosed as surra, a tropical blood disease, which some of the veterinary colonels at Kunming had known of old in the Philippines. It was thought that a serum for it was being developed in the U.S., and the vets radioed to see if they could get some by air. Meanwhile they waited, and it was a time of waiting generally. The first atom bomb went off about then and Jake began to feel the war was over, together with the mules' and his usefulness in it.

V–J Day came and went, and on August 20 the vets decided to shoot all positive mules in the first serial — they had been testing them and knew which were infected. Negative mules were handed at once to the Chinese. The aim was to keep the disease from spreading to the native mules and horses round Kunming, which besides being small were usually underfed and always without medical care — it was feared that anything bad enough to kill our mules might go through this native stock like wildfire, causing an international tragedy.

This feeling — that mules exposed to surra were better withheld than given to the Chinese — next began to apply to the second and third serials, especially after word came from home that no serum could be sent. It was hard to test the mules in these two serials, and to isolate them if infected, for they were in the country without the vet-hospital facilities of the FATC. Some were dying, perhaps one or two a day. Others were getting sick — losing weight and strength — and apparently heading for death, and often these were shot. Jake was detached from the argument that now developed — as to whether the mules should be wiped out *in toto* — since it was in the hands of Kunming's high-ranking veterinaries, especially of two top colonels; but he talked with these colonels almost daily and was in touch with their thoughts, and he concurred when they passed a general death sentence around September 1. Jake wasn't disappointed, really, nor were his colleagues of the trip so far as he could tell, in spite of the pains they had taken to bring the mules through. Most of them were now convinced, Jake says, that the mules couldn't fit easily into Chinese life — unless this was modified by a parallel GI war effort — even without their disease. Forcing them to fit in, it was believed, might be worse for them than a humane death. These views seem to have been in the Western tradition that leads us to shoot race horses with broken legs.

The death sentence was executed by men of Jake's party, from the second and third serials. It was a hard job because Army rules of hygiene demanded that the dead be buried at once. Jake went to Kunming's various plush headquarters in search of bulldozers or steam shovels, with operators — there was a great deal of such heavy stuff around then. But the roomfuls of colonels, their imaginations dulled by peace, couldn't visualize what he was up against this time, and they turned him down. He wondered how long one hundred men — all he had left now — would take to bury five hundred mules. He wondered how many of the hundred would have gone home before the task was done. He wondered where to get one hundred shovels. But then some of the men, riding in the hills above Kilo 51, found deep gullies there — a common thing in China, where deforestation and erosion are prevalent curses. Jake went up with them and saw that each gully would hold a few dozen carcasses, and then they found the same thing in the hills near Tsuyung. So he stopped asking for bulldozers and settled for a big store of dynamite and a bewildered young engineer lieutenant with a sergeant. The mules were shot in the gullies by crews of four or five men, armed with forty-fives and carbines, and then the two engineers blew the sides in over them with the dynamite.

After the mules' death the men went their ways, most of them to be attached to the Chinese artillery awhile and then sent home. Jake lingered in China for a month or so, long enough to observe that Sausser, when his mules were gone and he was transferred to Hostel 9, managed to bring his strawberry roan with him. Jake saw it there, hobbled outside in the hostel's well-kept front yard, while the strains of "Oh, That Strawberry Roan" and other cowboy songs floated through the window. As for the few live mules — the ones that got away uninfected from the first serial — Jake doesn't know their fate, though a friend of his saw American mules with the Chinese Army in 1947 at Changchun, Manchuria — over fifteen hundred miles northeast of Kunming as the crow flies. Even if these were the ones, though, which is doubtful, Jake thinks their fate must sooner or later have been that of their brothers: death in a strange land with the obscure fame of being the widest, and perhaps the last, world travelers of their kind. If fame like that means anything to mules.

A Walk with Vinoba

VINOBA BHAVE, the holy man who walks through India begging land for the poor, was camped near a grove of mangoes when I caught up with him recently. He himself was quartered in a schoolhouse, that is, but most of his followers were in tents under the trees. Mangoes have thick foliage high above the ground, and they cast a solid, airy shade most welcome on a hot day, as this was turning out to be. I arrived at eleven, and the party had been there since eight, having walked from their last camp in the early morning. They had eaten breakfast and washed up, and they were now sitting around writing letters, filling in records or taking it easy. Mostly they were men or boys and wore dhotis — loincloths — with shirts or nothing at all above the waist. They sat in tents or on bamboo mats in the shade. They received me hospitably and put my things in a tent that was assigned, I learned, to members of the national Bhoodan, or "Land Gift," movement, which has grown up round Vinoba in the past four years. I was told that another tent there belonged to the Orissa branch of the movement — the local chapter, that is, for Orissa State, the part of East India where we were now traveling. A third tent was for the Orissa Government, a fourth was for girls and a fifth for the bookstore — the party had a supply of Bhoodan literature along, which it put on sale at the stops. I gathered that the enterprise had swollen a good deal since Vinoba had begun it, in 1951, as virtually a one-man walking tour. Partly this was natural growth, it seemed, and partly it was because we were on a main highway now and getting help from the Orissa authorities. At this camp site two trucks, two jeeps and some bicycles were parked under the mangoes, and a number of black tin trunks were stacked here and there. The party was approaching the coastal town of Puri, where an annual get-together of Bhoodan enthusiasts was scheduled, and I learned that some of these had been joining up to walk for the final few days. This made for extra numbers and a holiday atmosphere that I gathered was not quite typical.

I settled in the tent and passed the time till noon, when a bell rang and we went to a nearby mat shelter for lunch. There we sat in rows on the ground and ate rice with two or three kinds of stewed vegetables. Afterward I slept for a couple of hours, as did most of the others — it was very hot — and at four o'clock I followed the crowd to a larger mango grove near by, where prayers were to be held and Vinoba was to speak. I was by now in the hands of a young Bhoodan worker named Sharma, whom I took to calling Sharmaji, the suffix "ji" being a friendly honorific in India — Vinoba, for instance, is always called Vinobaji by his followers (with the accent on the third syllable). Sharmaji led me to a space before a dais in this other mango grove, where some bamboo mats and tarpaulins had been spread on the ground, and we sat there while the crowd gathered. Sharmaji opened up a little portable spinning wheel he had with him and began spinning cotton yarn, a ritual activity promoted in India by Mahatma Gandhi — "Gandhiji" — and still practiced by his more devoted followers, among whom the Bhoodan people are numbered. Other Bhoodan workers arrived, sat down near us and began spinning too. Their wheels made a faint droning sound. The sun was low by now, and it was cool again under the trees. A strong wind came up, rustling them and filling the air with leaves and dust. Then it died down again. Our own space was roped off, and many of the local peasants were now crowded around it, the women wearing bright Indian dresses — saris — and much jewelry: nose rings, forearm bracelets and the like. A young Orissa Bhoodan worker sat cross-legged on a corner of the dais and kept the people occupied by talking over a public-address system — Sharmaji told me he was speaking Oriya, the local language, or dialect. He would talk on for a while, saying I don't know what, and then lead cheers for Gandhiji, Vinobaji and Bhoodan.

After a longish wait Vinobaji appeared, walking from

the camp site, with a small group of followers, male and female. He was a slight figure wearing a dhoti, and a white cotton shawl over his head and shoulders. The shawl was gathered at his throat, and above it a whitish-gray beard came out. He had an aquiline nose and horn-rimmed glasses. Nose, beard and glasses were about all you could see of his face. His walk was light and springy. He mounted the dais, kicked off his sandals and sat down cross-legged on a low table there, which was covered by a green quilt and green cloth. He kept on sitting quietly, as if lost in meditation — rocking a little and working his mouth at times — while a few women of the party led chanted prayers, which came over the public-address system with very good musical effect, I thought. They lasted for half an hour, or a good part of that, and during them the spinning kept up undiminished. When they were over Vinobaji looked around, shifted his position a little, and got ready to talk. He was gentle, attractive and quiet, and his voice was gentle too — not insistent or aggressive. He seemed a fine, light-boned man, but well muscled — his bare arms came out under the shawl, which covered his trunk and shoulders. Later I learned he had done manual work for years, as part of his religious life and service to the villagers. His skin had a healthy glow. His hands were delicate, and he made quiet gestures with them. He spoke in Hindi — India's national language — and a young local man translated into Oriya. Vinoba would speak briefly — for about fifteen seconds — and then pause for the interpreter. The latter's voice was loud and brash. Vinoba's was gentle but serious. He was expounding, teaching, laying down the line. He had a folded cloth like a napkin in one hand, and now and then he tapped it with the other for emphasis.

He began, I found out later, with a reference to Puri, which is a famous goal of pilgrimage in India and the site of a famous temple. He said he was on his way to Puri, but not to worship God in the temple there. He preferred to find God in a temple made by God himself, namely man. God was surely in this temple, he said, and could be found by kindness. He talked on, and soon he asked his listeners to give one sixth of their land to the landless — one sixth being his usual demand, based on the argument that the poor should be treated as another child in the family, of whom there may be five already as things go in India. The difference between men and beasts, Vinoba said, is that men need not quarrel with each other. He said God forgives sinners, but men who are unkind cannot approach God. And he continued in this vein, I gathered — stressing the religious duty to give — while the big red tropical sun went down behind him. He talked for upward of half an hour.

Later he autographed several copies, by request, of some sermons on the Bhagavad Gita, the Hindu "Bible," which he had preached while in jail in 1932, in Gandhi's non-co-operation movement — these are said to be very popular in India. Then he left, and his workers called out for land gifts, and countrymen in dhotis came forward and made some, which were recorded on a simple form amid shouts and cheers.

I was introduced to Vinobaji that evening, as he sat cross-legged on a low platform outside his schoolhouse billet. It was dark and his head was still covered by the shawl, like the head of a European peasant woman. Again, my chief impression was of beard and glasses. We had no conversation to speak of — later I learned he is rather deaf — but he was gracious and made me at home.

I did little else that evening but eat dinner — it was much the same as lunch — and take to my sleeping bag early. I was awakened once in the night when jackals invaded our camp. They made unearthly howls, and as I listened in the dark it seemed as if an intangible force had flowed in among us. Then it flowed away again. I went back to sleep and was next awakened by the rising bell at three o'clock — it was a handbell shaken by one of the party, who went from tent to tent. I dressed at once and busied myself with packing — luckily there was good light from a late half moon — and as I did so a face appeared at the tent flap and asked about my impression of the Bhoodan movement. I said it impressed me greatly, and meanwhile I fumbled with my things.

"There are two principles in Indian thought," the face said. "One is sacrifice within enjoyment. The other is enjoyment within sacrifice." The face, which seemed disembodied in the moonlight, began explaining about

Indian gods who had everything — money, women, and so forth — but were still detached, and about others — he mentioned Shiva for one — who suffered and made sacrifices and got supreme enjoyment thereby. "We are followers of Shiva," the face said, and added that Gandhiji had been the same and so had Swami Vivekananda, a famous Hindu reformer of the late nineteenth century. "These men got their enjoyment from renunciation, sacrifice, doing good for others," the face declared, and then it disappeared. It just dematerialized, and I never identified it again in the party.

At half past three prayers began outside Vinobaji's schoolhouse, and I went there after putting my baggage in a pile by a truck. Vinobaji sat cross-legged on his low platform, and his followers sat facing him on the ground, cross-legged too, in rows in the moonlight. Women led the chanting again, and to me it seemed beautiful. It lasted half an hour, and then we rose and began the day's walk immediately. Vinobaji led and the rest of us followed — thirty-odd of us in an irregular column (others were to catch up later, I learned, in the jeeps and trucks). Vinobaji stepped along briskly, talking somewhat with his neighbors to right and left. I stayed back — say in the third or fourth row of the column — and talked with Sharmaji and others of my new friends, or walked in silence. There were a half dozen kerosene lamps in the crowd. Once or twice we met cars, but they pulled into the ditch and doused their lights, evidently recognizing and respecting us. We hurried on past them. Thus we proceeded for an hour, and then on the dot of five we stopped, and two of Vinobaji's helpers, a boy and girl, mixed him a concoction of milk, honey and yoghurt from a thermos, and other containers, that they had with them. I was told this was his sole diet now, partly because of an ulcer. He was given the mixture in a thermos-flask top and ate it with a big spoon. We set out again when we had finished.

During the second hour dawn came up, and at six we moved off the road and into a field, where the party sat down in concentric circles to hear Vinoba read from the Hindu classics in Oriya, which he had, according to Sharmaji, been studying since entering Orissa two months earlier — he is a famed linguist and scholar. He sat in the middle of the group, facing a couple of Oriya literati who were traveling with us; and he read aloud, questioned, and made jokes, these drawing laughs from the encircling followers. The session lasted an hour, during which the red sun rose and at least a hundred villagers gathered round us curiously. At the end there was a short prayer; Vinobaji had more milk, yoghurt and honey; and we took to the road again.

Eight o'clock — with the sun now warm — found us in the outskirts of Bhubaneshwar, a town that was to be our night's halt, and a crowd came out to join us. I found myself walking with a young businessman who was pushing a bicycle. He was pleasant, with a strong face and a mustache. He asked my views on the Bhoodan movement and then volunteered that he believed idle or absentee landlords — nonproductive ones — should give up their land, but questioned whether working ones should be pressed to do so. He wondered if production — so important in India — wouldn't fall off in this case, and he questioned whether small holdings were really efficient. "Only the bigger farmers," he said, "have means to improve their tools and stock." I found out later that land-reform legislation was being debated in Orissa at the time, and that feelings on the matter were running high in some quarters. Yet this young businessman seemed calm in his criticisms, and he seemed to admire Vinoba and the movement. We walked on, watching the crowd thicken. People were scurrying on the flanks now, straining for a sight of Vinobaji. "Only a man of great moral strength can lead the masses in India," my acquaintance said, and soon after that we parted. The crowd pressed on us more and more, trying to see Vinobaji and to garland him with flowers. Then we reached a school compound where we were to spend the night.

I walked for six days with Vinoba's party, and stayed for another week in Puri while he was there, and all this time I wondered about his hold on the people, and about the morale of his workers, both of which seemed remarkable. The problem of land — how to take it from the haves and give it to the have-nots — is thought to be one of the worst things afflicting Asia now, and in some countries, notably China, the idea has prevailed that you can solve it only by killing landlords. Yet here was

Vinoba solving it gently, or at least making a start that way. In four years, I was told, he and his followers had collected gifts totaling three million seven hundred thousand acres. Much of this was wasteland, or land with unclear title, but much was also good, I gathered, and Vinoba was talking of greater things to come — of fifty million good acres, or one sixth of the arable land in India, by the end of 1957. This seemed an ambitious goal, yet for all one could see he might make it. Intangible, psychological factors seemed to be in play, defying analysis. Vinoba himself had been the best prophet about his movement so far — he had steadily confounded skeptics by doing what he said he would do. I wondered how this had happened. And I wondered what kept his followers going in a life that seemed hard even under these comparatively de luxe conditions of the Puri road.

The core of these followers, I gathered from Sharmaji as the days passed, were old-time Gandhian "constructive workers." Gandhi, it seemed, had promoted two main activities — politics and "constructive work" — in his movement. The former was being carried on now under Pandit Nehru by the Indian Congress Party, which was enjoying the satisfactions of leadership in the newly free country. But the latter, comprising less glamorous things like rural education, public-health work and the encouragement of handicrafts — village uplift, by and large — had gone into a slump after Gandhi's death in 1948; public interest had lagged, and the constructive workers had felt isolated and leaderless. "They didn't know what to do," Sharmaji said, "until Vinobaji started the Bhoodan movement." He had done this in 1951, and since then the constructive workers — numbering eight or nine thousand altogether — had concentrated on Bhoodan more and more, often leaving their village schools, clinics, and so on, for the purpose. What I was seeing, then, was this side of Gandhiism in its current phase; and Vinoba, I soon learned, was Gandhi's heir where it was concerned. He was fully entitled to this role, in the judgment of Sharmaji and the rest, having been a star Gandhi disciple for thirty years — indeed they tended to argue that he, rather than Nehru, was the principal heir, and in support they cited the fact that Gandhi had sent Vinoba out first, and Nehru second, to court arrest in 1942, when the decision had been made to oppose the British war effort. They ridiculed the Congress — and politicians — a good deal, as being corrupt and flabby, and they left no doubt that they thought themselves the true believers. They were the bearers of the Gandhian cult, one might say, and their more important ceremonies, like the spinning and the prayers, had come down unchanged from Gandhi's time.

As seen in the party, the constructive workers appeared to be earnest, idealistic people of all ages from the late teens up. A few were picturesque. One was a handsome, merry young man, broad-shouldered and well muscled as he stood in his dhoti, with a mop of curly black hair and big curly black beard — he looked like a satyr, and he used to tend a recording machine during

Vinobaji's talks. Another was a bald, stooped, but cheerful oldster carrying a big staff like those of the sages in Oriental paintings. A third was a sturdy muscle-man — a solemn puritan, I judged him — who insisted on carrying his own baggage all the way, while the rest of us walked free. These few stood out; the others were normal clean-looking altruists such as one might expect in a YMCA gathering at home — except, of course, that they were Indians. Girls, or women, were in the minority — no more than twenty-five per cent of the total. They wore homespun saris whereas the men, by and large, wore homespun dhotis, nearly always plain white in color. Washing these clothes was one of the first tasks when we had reached a new stop and had finished breakfast. A bathing place would be screened off for the women, but as a rule the men would wash out of doors, in public, with their dhotis on. They would sluice themselves down thoroughly at a pump or a bucket and would then, as I got it, put on a clean dhoti and hang the wet one out as wash — dhotis are simple oblongs of cloth, without stitches even, and adepts not only can wash them easily, but can apparently put them on and take them off anywhere with modesty. So man and clothing would get clean together. This procedure was hard for me to adapt to, as I was wearing a shirt and khaki shorts, and I am afraid I was rather dirty much of the time. Another hard thing to learn was kicking my shoes off when I entered a tent or mat shelter — Indians do this customarily, and they wear slippers or sandals that lend themselves to

it. Then there was the cross-legged sitting. My feet go
to sleep if I sit motionless that way for long, as I learned
to my regret one morning at prayers — after that I sat
on the outskirts where I could shift without making a
disturbance. At meals there was nothing against my
shifting my legs frequently. Everyone else at these meals
ate with his simple right hand, unaided, but I couldn't
do this — at least with any speed — and one of the Bhoodan workers thoughtfully lent me a spoon. The food was
ladled out onto our banana leaves from buckets, by
volunteer waiters, as we sat in our rows. Some rice was
put on the leaf first and then the rest was ladled on top of
this, unless you specified otherwise. Then you mixed
everything together, into a mush, and ate it. The food
was all vegetarian. I thought it was good, if simple,
though I suppose I might have tired of it eventually. I
liked the breakfasts especially — a typical one might include unpolished rice with yoghurt, molasses, shredded
coconut and coarse salt put on it. This was really deli-
cious when mixed together. Fruit might be put down
on the edge of your leaf as well — a banana, perhaps —
and there might even be some spice, say a bit of ginger.
I gathered that we were living high by ordinary Bhoodan
standards, and that this was a display of local pride by
our hosts — the comparatively rich villages on the highway.

Sharmaji told me there were many smaller Bhoodan
parties now traveling in India in imitation of Vinoba's —
in extension of his idea. He, Sharmaji, had been doing

this work himself till a few weeks earlier, when he had
dropped it to set out for the Puri conference. He said
a party might number three or four people, young men
as a rule, though girls were useful too if they could be
fitted in — they could, for instance, enter houses and
get the women to coax their husbands into giving land.
The parties always walked, and each member carried his
own things, which meant traveling light — a thin blanket roll, a knapsack and the small spinning wheel were
about all one could handle. A party would waken early
in a given village and start right away for the next one,
perhaps two or three miles distant. There they would
get all the men together as soon as possible, would explain about Bhoodan and ask for gifts, and would pass
the noon hour, usually being fed by the villagers. Then
they would rest awhile — India is a siesta country — and
would walk on to the next stop, perhaps two or three
miles farther away, holding another meeting that evening. The routine varied — a party might deal with only
one village in a day, because of delays — but this was the
general idea.

Many of the Bhoodan workers came from white-collar
backgrounds, and I gathered they were committing themselves to a life of walking, sleeping on hard floors and
eating Indian peasant fare, which is notoriously poor. It
sounded to me like knighthood when in flower, or like
the early Christian religious orders, and I wondered
about the workers' motives. I knew that Gandhi himself
had said his life effort was a search for God, primarily,

and that any other motive one might see in it — charitable, reformist, and so on — was subsidiary to this. And while with the Bhoodan party I found similar statements by Vinoba (I was reading his translated speeches as we went along). Both men seemed to look on their self-sacrifice as a way of perfecting themselves spiritually — drawing nearer to God — and I gathered this was in line with the Hindu religious tradition, which stresses asceticism, and selflessness, as a means of spiritual progress. The religious motive was discernible in the party as a whole, too, not only in the prayers, but in the general talk. One man in the company assured me that "this movement is led by God," and at other times I heard English phrases like "scientific religion" come popping out of Hindi conversations in our tent. There was everywhere an air of religious thought.

Yet this was not all, for some members of the group, Sharmaji included, seemed to be what we might call scientific humanists. Sharmaji called himself an atheist, in fact, and when I asked why he had joined the Gandhian movement he said it was because he had read deeply in writers like Carlyle, Ruskin, Tolstoy and Marx, and they had convinced him that service to mankind was his duty. Such reasoning, it seemed to me, was the same as leads young Western materialists into causes. Even so, Sharmaji seemed to believe in the process of conversion — what Christians might call "being born again" — which I found to be another feature of the movement. Many, if not all, of the Bhoodan workers felt that their characters changed for the better after being in the work for a while — often they discussed this in a matter-of-fact way. Many believed, too, that the presence of Vinoba — his spiritual influence — could work a rapid change of this sort in those who were exposed to it. Sharmaji accepted this belief, for all his atheism, though he had not experienced the influence himself. He told me in explanation that he had already been much changed — before meeting Vinobaji — by another leading constructive worker, an outstanding personality, with whom he had been associated for a long time. He seemed to feel this had left less room, in his case, for Vinoba's spiritual power to manifest itself. To me his beliefs seemed an odd mixture of the spiritual and the material, yet there they were.

Sharmaji was an energetic man of about thirty, with a postgraduate degree in biology. He was always active and restless in the camp, saying he missed the hard work of the smaller land-gift parties. While the rest of us sat round he came and went constantly, singing to himself in a high, penetrating voice, and he talked profusely and vigorously in English, using long words like "utilize." He was apt to say "definitely" rather than "yes." He also spun yard after yard of thread in his odd moments, and it was he who explained to me about the spinning wheel, or charkha, which was so much a symbol of the movement. His own charkha was of a common type, neat and portable and contained in a trim, polished, dark-stained wooden box about nine by eighteen by four inches — a little over these dimensions, if anything. When opened up it seemed like a very small portable phonograph. Sharmaji sat beside it on the ground, cranking a wheel in it with his right hand and holding the thread, plus a wisp of raw cotton, in his left. He told me his charkha had cost thirteen rupees and eight annas — about three American dollars. He said he spun thread for forty yards of cloth each year, which was his own consumption. Every Bhoodan worker was supposed to spin for at least half an hour a day, which would make enough thread for about twenty yards yearly. It was expected that all the workers would wear homespun cloth, called khadi, in their clothing — dhotis, saris, shawls, long Indian shirts, and so on. This put its mark on the group's appearance, for the khadi was both rough and rather flimsy-looking. Its superiority to machine-spun cotton lay mainly in the ideological field, so far as I could tell. Gandhiji had first promoted khadi as a form of economic warfare, on behalf of the Indian village, against the Lancashire cotton mills, and now, after independence, it was being continued as warfare, still on behalf of the village, against big mills in India as well as abroad — against the whole capitalist or machine-age system, really, not just colonialism. As warfare it had its handicaps. Sharmaji told me that khadi had to be hand woven as well as hand spun, because the thread wasn't strong enough for machine looms. He also said it wore out soon if you gave it to professional launderers, and he had long followed the rule of washing all his things himself.

I picked up this lore as Sharmaji and I sat together, on a tarpaulin, before the afternoon prayer sessions. He would spin as we talked, and other Bhoodan workers would sit down near us, open their charkhas and spin too. Some of the less-experienced young men had a hard time. Their thread would keep snapping or bunching up, and they would have almost nothing to show for an afternoon's work. The girls seemed much better, on an average, and I mused that Chinese — great masters of fine work — might also be better than Indians on the whole. Yet this was beside the point. The spinning seemed fully as much an exercise as a practical pursuit, if not more so. It bound the workers into the movement with dramatic symbolism, and it guaranteed that they would have some quiet time each day for reflection — perhaps coinciding with the prayers, perhaps not.

Vinobaji lived apart as we traveled. Sometimes he would stay in a schoolhouse while we were in tents near by. Or if we all went into a school compound he would be given a special corner of it. He would have a room, and outside it his portable wooden platform — about the size of a bed, but lower — would be set up. He would conduct early morning prayers from this, and in the evening he would sit cross-legged there and receive callers — the big afternoon prayer-and-talk session would be held elsewhere, at a slight distance. He didn't walk through the camp unless his route to or from this session led him there. Then if you met him he would have a few

cheerful words for you. His manner was light and hu-
morous — debonair — and a meeting with him made you
feel good. He was, I think, very busy. When we arrived
at a new place — say at eight in the morning — he would
bathe, have some of his yoghurt mixture, and then study
Oriya for two hours with a young schoolteacher who had
joined the party for this purpose. After that he would
have people to see, and correspondence to deal with, besides getting some rest in the noon heat — he was, after all,
an invalid, though one tended to forget this; his ulcer
had immobilized him for several weeks in the past year.

When I joined the party he had two temporary secretaries with him — a young man and a girl — and a woman
attendant called Mahadevi Tai, or Sister Mahadevi (his
regular secretary, an older, experienced man, was away
then, but rejoined us later). I gathered that Mahadevi
Tai had served Vinobaji in his ashram, or religious re-
treat, for a long time before the Bhoodan movement
started. She was a thin, middle-aged woman with glasses,
plain but very likable. Devoted care of Vinobaji seemed
to be her whole mission in life. She did not walk while
I was along — she rode in a jeep — but she had walked
thousands of miles before that. She often accompanied
Vinobaji in public and did things like giving him a hand
when he stepped up onto the lecture dais. She was one of
half a dozen people who habitually sat on the dais during
his afternoon talks. There was also the girl secretary, taking shorthand; an interpreter for Oriya; one or two
senior Gandhian disciples of the party; and a musician

named Dukhayal — Dukhayalji — who was apt to arrive early and lead the crowd in some songs he had composed. Dukhayalji was a refugee from Pakistan and seemed a natural trouper — I would call him one of the less solemn members of the group, though he was as tough as anyone when it came to walking and leading the camp life. His songs, which he accompanied on a tambourine, were rousing ones about Bhoodan and Vinobaji.

A good deal of Vinoba's hold on the masses, I gathered in time, came simply from his being a religious man by profession. This is the most honorable career in India, one always hears, and those who observe its forms are often venerated even if they are really disreputable and vicious. Vinoba was neither, of course, but had lived an unusually pure life. He had followed Gandhi since 1916, spending most of his time in the austere routine of ashrams, while studying and working on problems of village welfare. Before starting the Bhoodan movement, I was told, he had been known as a scholarly recluse, very shy and strict, though he had blossomed out a good deal now that he was a public figure. In his ashram days he had become one of the greatest living scholars of Hinduism, and an expert on Christianity and Islam too. To study Islam he had learned Arabic. He had also, through the years, learned six or eight Indian languages as well as French and, of course, English. His mastery of the Hindu scriptures plainly came in handy now. In his talks — as I found by reading old ones and having new ones summarized by Sharmaji — he frequently dealt with local religious figures or legends. Not uncommonly he began an afternoon's talk by quoting something the people of that place had said to him in the morning, and at times the latter would have used scripture to question his teachings, which were radical theologically as well as economically. He would have no trouble with such questions. He would simply make his own interpretation of the point — usually a more profound and better-informed one than that of his critics — and would carry the day.

I have been told that Gandhi's approach to religion was intuitive, whereas Vinoba's was more intellectual. Gandhi was a political reformer, searching for ways to advance his cause, and this led him to religion naturally. Vinoba, on the other hand, started out as a religious scholar, and this led him in the end to political action. He is said to have had unusual powers of reason and logic even as a young man, together with a prodigious memory and will, and a strong temper. His will helped him to live on the low peasant level — to support himself entirely by spinning at times, and to make arduous experiments in vegetable growing. He drove himself so hard at the spinning that he is now rated the most skillful charkha operator in India. He once determined to spin an unbroken thread long enough for a whole yard of cloth and did so — his followers cite this as a heroic feat of perseverance.

Two things had been amiss in Indian public life, I gathered, when Vinoba had started Bhoodan. One — the frustration of the Gandhian constructive workers — we have noted already. The other was an outbreak of Communist violence in rural India, especially in a southern region called Telengana. The Reds had begun organizing the peasants there, and killing and terrorizing landlords. Then the government had moved in troops and begun a counterterror, whereupon landlords and Red suspects had gone in fear alternately, by night and by day. This had been all wrong by Gandhian principles, which teach that violence never solves anything. It had also been a challenge to Gandhian leadership by an alien morality, whose principle of land reform had nevertheless been worthy in Gandhian eyes — the landholdings in Telengana had been huge, I learned, and the landless there very poor. Thus some proof had been called for that Indian culture could adjust its own inequities, and Vinoba doubtless had this in mind when he walked into Telengana — in April of 1951 — with a few followers. He seems to have made very little fuss, but to have just wandered around talking with the people in a friendly way. During these talks some paupers had told him they needed land — could get nowhere without it — and at a gathering right after that he had asked if someone would give it to them. A man had spoken up at once, offering a hundred acres, and Vinoba had taken this as a sign from God and had gone ahead with his movement from there. Its growth to its present state — with Bhoodan workers all over the country and a record of three million seven hundred thousand acres in gifts — had been in a smooth enough progression, I gathered, but spotted with episodes that were already part of a legend. For instance, when Vinoba's early success had become known, Pandit Nehru had invited him to New Delhi for conferences. Vinoba had accepted, but had walked all the way, taking several weeks, and when he had reached the capital had settled down to living in a tent there. This gesture had dramatized the difference between his ways and those of officialdom, and it had been in a time-honored Asian style. Asian history is full of sages who have scorned titular power, yet have exerted great temporal influence by their austerity — some of the Old Testament prophets are examples. Vinoba seemed to fill this ancient role.

The trouble in Telengana had subsided, thanks in large part to Bhoodan, and now in 1955 India was without Communist disorders, rural or otherwise. So far as I knew there were various reasons for this, but Bhoodan was certainly a main one. It wasn't that Bhoodan had solved the land problem — it had thus far collected only a small fraction of India's good acreage; and only a small fraction of this, in turn, had been distributed. But it had put the finger of scorn on violence, that basic Communist weapon, and it had absorbed much of the nation's youthful idealism. This last seemed important. Through the years I had often heard the strength of Asian communism laid to the peasants, but I had long concluded that the idealistic young people were more really the prime mover — that it was they who dedicated themselves most wholly to the cause, and they who led the peasants (who would, in fact, be helpless by themselves).

Now I saw that Vinoba gave an alternative to communism, and a patriotic one, for young Indians who could not abide their society as it was.

I had only one formal interview with Vinoba, and it was not too satisfactory. It was after we had reached Puri — to get ahead of the story for a moment — and he was beset by important visitors from all over India. Perhaps I shouldn't have pressed to see him then, but I did, and was received one morning. I found him sitting in his room, on the floor, with several other callers. He was dressed only in a loin-cloth and was spinning on a very light charkha. All the callers — six or eight — were seated at his right side, because he is deaf in his left ear, and I settled down among them, cross-legged and shoeless. I had sent a note ahead — also because of his deafness — asking him to answer just one question: how the principles of nonviolence might be propagated in the West.

Vinoba was silent for a moment after I had sat down, and then he repeated the question I had written and added: "Which is East and which is West?"

"Say Europe and America are the West," I answered, and then changed. "Say the West is the part where nonviolence is not such a strong idea."

"I don't think it is that way," he said. "They have their Bible. The thing to do is not to read it one day and forget about it the other six." He paused. "They are all afraid," he said — or I thought he said; he was murmuring in a low voice that was hard to catch. "We should find out the reason for their fear." Then he paused again, for a long time. I was waiting for him, but apparently he was waiting for me. He kept looking away to his left side, which was necessary because of the spinning, yet it seemed to draw his attention off from us at the right. Finally I was nudged by his secretary.

"How to find out the reason for the fear," I said.

There was another pause, and Vinoba muttered something about "strongest country in the world . . . have everything . . . why should they be afraid?" (He meant America.) Another pause. I said there was a habit in the West now of expecting attack from others — that this had been intensified during the past fifteen years or so. He didn't understand me, apparently, and when the others tried to enlighten him, in Hindi, it seemed that they didn't understand either. The whole conversation broke down, really, with misunderstanding, Vinoba looking the other way and I not knowing whether to leave or not.

"Well, then," I finally said, "what the West should do is follow Christian principles more closely?"

Vinoba agreed it was. "Love thy neighbor as thyself," he murmured as he spun. And then I took my leave.

Several reasons could be advanced why the interview had turned out this way — my own style of approach could have been one. Even so, I felt Vinoba had ignored many things relevant to the question, though it was not one he disclaimed competence on. He had ignored many developments since Christ that had affected the Western mind, or so I thought — the long European tradition of conflict, to name just one. His approach to the question had seemed pedantic to me, and whereas I had formerly looked for some universal light from him I was now inclined to pigeonhole him more strictly as an Indian cult hero. Yet my admiration for his intellect was still great. I had been reading his translated speeches right along, and they seemed beautifully argued to me, and economical of rhetoric.

He was not a practical man, I judged. So far as I could learn on the trip only a small fraction — less than ten per cent — of the land thus far donated had actually been passed on to the poor, and a good organization for doing this had not been built up yet. Bhoodan workers seemed to drift hither and yon as they saw fit. They had little supervision. This went with Vinoba's ideas, for he was firmly opposed to centralization. Yet I didn't see how his already vast landholdings — plus gifts of money, equipment, and so forth, that were coming in too — could be handled that way for long.

Then his economics — based in part on Gandhi's — struck me as questionable. Gandhiji had maintained that the Indian village had been a relative paradise till corrupted by British cloth and other machine products. This had been a useful idea in the freedom struggle, but it had not accomplished any return to paradise after independence. The villages were still very poor affairs (as a non-Gandhian outsider might guess they always had been). Vinoba's cure for the evil, so far as I could tell, was to carry Gandhiism still farther, with relentless, if narrow-

minded, logic. Not only was he all-out for charkhas,
handlooms, khadi, and so forth, but he had also experimented in his own ashram for years, before starting
Bhoodan, with a moneyless village economy. On first
joining his party I had assumed that the goal of fifty million acres in land gifts — one sixth of India's arable soil,
taken from the rich and given to the poor — was the limit
of his ambition. But I found this wasn't true, on getting
into his speeches. His ultimate plan was that *no* land in
India would be in private hands. All villages would be
owned and run co-operatively. The role of money would
be curtailed, and every Indian would be required to do
manual work. Vinoba also wanted to abolish political
parties, and expected that the formal state structure
would wither away — to borrow a Communist phrase —
in the face of his village co-operative society. Indeed his
program seemed fully as revolutionary as the Communists', and the Bhoodan drive was but a step toward its
realization.

Each morning we drew nearer the coast, in our walk,
and as we did so the landscape took on more of a South
Seas look. Palm trees began to dominate, making for a
Gauguin, or Rousseau, quality. Their leaves were dark
and threw a dark shade, in contrast to the glare and
tawny grass of the fields behind us. We felt salt in the
air, and more moisture. The land itself grew wetter, in
fact, with more ponds, these often covered by water
hyacinths — mats of greenery spotted with lavender-

blue flowers. We could see these changes every day, the dawn finding us in a slightly new environment. The villages grew bigger and richer too. They would be dressed up to receive us. There would be fresh white writing, or pictures, on the brown walls, and before each door would be set a special offering: some grains of rice with a cook pot resting on them, this smeared with red powder, then some mango leaves on the pot's mouth and a coconut atop the nest thus formed. It was a standard Indian welcome sign, according to Sharmaji. The people in the village would wait by the road to see us, the women greeting us with a queer yodeling wail that was peculiar to Orissa.

The crowds in the afternoons grew bigger, and hawkers came to sell them things, till each day's gathering was almost like a fair. Usually a couple of teashops were set up, which was a boon to me — tea being a luxury not enjoyed within the movement — and I would slip out in the afternoon and have some. Many of the peasants came in bullock carts, parking them by the roadside. The carts had high wheels and vaulted covers of bamboo matting, shaped like those on our own covered wagons, but much smaller. The bullocks were humped and cream colored, with big horns curving above their heads. They seemed very gentle as they stood there — like all the cattle in India indeed, where bulls wander harmlessly — nonviolently — in the city streets.

I never really plumbed the crowd's attitude about giving, or that of the public at large. The bosom of the movement was no place to explore this, in fact — all those around me, Sharmaji and the rest, seemed blinded toward it by their enthusiasm. Yet I struck up an acquaintance with an official who was traveling with us from duty, having been ordered to keep a watch on things. He was a portly young man, intelligent but plainly self-indulgent by the standards of that company. He would lag far behind in the morning walks, and sometimes I would join him. He told me many people were uneasy because Vinoba talked only of collection, and not much of distribution; they wondered what would become of all the donated land. I asked him about pressure being put on landowners to give — of which there are many tales in India — and he said there was some of this, certainly, but he felt it was still possible to withhold land in most places, though he didn't know how long that would last. "It's a question of sentiment now," he said. "Who are sentimental are giving. Who are hypocritical are retaining. People aren't all the same." After which he fell silent, plodding on through the dawn.

The last prayer meeting was held on an expanse of green grass, smooth and closely grazed, almost like a lawn. Rows of palms stood up from it, and there were some bamboos round the edge. The crowd was normal — a few thousand people, that is, the men in dhotis, the women sitting apart in bright saris, the children squirming. Vinoba came, mounted the dais and sat down. The prayers were chanted. Then he began his gentle, patient talk. I strolled off to one end of the ground, beyond the crowd, and there met an elderly Bhoodan worker who was pacing back and forth like a peripatetic philosopher. He told me Vinoba was saying that there are two kinds of people — those who believe evil can be overcome and those who don't, and who don't think reform is worth while. The old man paced on again, and I strolled away in another direction. I looked back at the main scene. There was green grass below and green palm leaves above, and in between was the crowd itself, a horizontal band of spotted color, seen through the gray palm trunks in the soft afternoon light. With it went an accompaniment of voices on the loud-speaker — the quiet one of Vinoba and the brisk one of the interpreter, alternating. After a while my course met that of the old man again, and he told me Vinoba was talking about love. We all have love for our families, he was saying, and he asked that this be broadened into love for the whole village. Science was in favor of love; it decreed that we must love each other — do each other no harm — if we are to survive. And all the great teachers had taught the same thing. We had all experienced love ourselves, Vinoba said, but we must broaden it, and that was all he asked. Whereupon he ended, then signed a few copies of his sermons and left, and his helpers began calling out for land gifts.

The next day we walked into Puri, which turned out to be a big town, with huge crowds awaiting us. Vinoba walked right past them, head high, at a brisk pace, and he kept this up through a mile or two of streets, till he reached the quarters assigned to him. A few days later he moved to a bamboo-mat encampment that had been built for the conference. It was a huge affair, set on an expanse of sand dunes outside the city, and six or eight thousand visitors, from all over India, came to stay there. It seemed to be very well planned. The mass serving of vegetarian food was excellent, and there were innumerable water outlets where the guests could bathe and wash their clothes. There was an exhibit area, with stalls showing things like khadi, plus many posters likening Vinoba to the Buddha and Gandhiji. The center of interest, however, was a pandal, or open shelter, with a matting roof on uprights, that shaded a great rectangle of sand — almost an acre, I would guess. It had a platform in the middle of one side, and there Vinoba sat with other dignitaries — including Rajendra Prasad, the Indian President — during the formal conference sessions. Thousands of people attended these sessions, and hundreds sat spinning in the pandal at other times. It was the constructive workers' big annual get-together, and Vinoba was the star. He did not disappoint. In his opening speech he ridiculed politics and urged officials to resign and take up Bhoodan work if they wished to help their country. And in his closing speech, two days later, he said he aspired to achieve a stateless society in India by 1957. He said he was God's instrument in this. He declared that by '57 world peace would be a reality and he raised his hand up, its fingers cupped and pointing skyward, as if holding this prize. His listeners were plainly much affected, and many Indians have since left other work for Bhoodan. Many have thorough faith in his predictions too, I think, though I cannot tell if they are right.

The Jungle Stalker

Here and there in Asia one always hears about the Gurkhas, the fighting men the British Army recruits from the Himalayan kingdom of Nepal. In India one sees the small forms of retired Gurkhas, now serving as watchmen, drawn up straight and smart before the city buildings. A Gurkha can be spotted not only by his bantam size, but by his very Oriental face, his stiff broad felt hat and his kukri, a heavy knife about twenty inches long and of peculiar shape. Kukris are the badge of the Gurkhas, who all carry them, as do their British officers, and a body of myths has grown up to embellish this fact. A kukri has a pair of small notches near the base of its blade, and one often hears that these are used for sighting before throwing the thing; one hears too that kukris may not be taken from their sheaths and put back unless blood is meanwhile drawn; but in truth they are never thrown, and they are taken out time and again without bleeding anything more noteworthy than a tin can or lead pencil; they are practical weapons that might be called the Gurkha's best friend. In the last war one heard often of Gurkhas attacking the Japanese in Burma with kukris alone, having run out of ammunition, and these stories were nearer the truth. The Gurkhas played a brave role in Burma, as they did in Africa and Italy, and had done before then on the North-West Frontier and in Egypt, Persia, Gallipoli and other places where the empire was threatened. They are one of the great mercenary fighting peoples of history.

For a long time I have wanted to learn more about the Gurkhas. I missed a chance in late 1949, when some were at Hong Kong in the garrison waiting there as the Chinese Reds came southward. The Reds were widely expected to attack Hong Kong, a small British colony, when they reached its border; but they failed to do so, and much of the garrison was shipped to other trouble spots like Malaya and Korea. Nearly all the British Gurkhas have been in Malaya since early 1950, helping keep down the jungle-based Red revolt there. In essence they make up four regiments of two battalions each (there were ten regiments to start with, but India took six in the recent partition). In Malaya the Gurkhas are scattered through the country, a four-hundred-mile peninsula beset by guerrillas, called "bandits," nearly everywhere. They have kept their fame there and added to it. While traveling in Malaya recently I talked with all kinds of people, from high commanders down, and they agreed that the Gurkhas were the best troops the British had

on hand for jungle warfare. In these travels too I satisfied my wish to learn some more about Gurkhas. I arranged to spend a few days with the 2/6 — the Second
Battalion of the Sixth Gurkha Rifles — which is in Johore,
the southernmost Malayan state, in a troublesome district
covered mainly by jungle checkered with rubber.

Soon after arriving at the battalion I found myself joining one of its patrols by evening dark. Malayan jungle
patrols stay out for long stretches, but they must be ra-
tioned anew each three days or so, and this is managed
by dark (if not by air drop) so the neighborhood will
have less chance to learn their whereabouts and tell the
bandits. I was in the care of a British lieutenant, and a
truck dropped us with the rations at a lonely point by a
hard road, where men from the patrol stood waiting.
There was a new moon and we could see after a fashion.
In the ditch the men sorted out the gear and got it on
their backs, and we set off through some rubber; it was
open and spaced in rows, and it allowed good walking
even in that light. After a few score yards we turned
onto a jungle path and before long came to the camp,
which was being pitched in an old clearing. There were
thirteen men in the patrol; one sat on sentry duty with a
Bren gun and the others busied with the rations and the
camp. They weren't too quiet; the lieutenant said ra-
tionings were nearly always spotted anyway, and made
known to the bandits, so a patrol's normal discipline was
slackened during them; more stress was put on getting
away quietly the next morning to new country — trying

to work there unbeknownst a couple of days. So muffled
banging, rattling and talking were heard. The moon shone
faintly in the clearing. The men made their beds on small
platforms of saplings; they hung a poncho, gabled like a
tent roof, over each of these and below it a mosquito net,
and inside they laid a blanket for warmth; most of them
customarily doubled up, I was told, to share equipment
and save carrying. When they were through that evening the camp looked like a hamlet of coffins.

Some rum had come in with us, a thing the Gurkhas
like, and we sat down to talk awhile before turning in.
The lieutenant and I sat with three of the men: his orderly, who spoke some English; a sergeant named Tekbahadur, who led the patrol; and another whom I cannot
place — I couldn't see faces at all that night. The Gurkhas
were free with the rum, which they said kept mosquitoes
off; unless you stopped them they filled your canteen cup
a third full at a pouring; and I have since learned that
openhandedness is a main Gurkha trait. The lieutenant
told me this patrol was a special ranger one, made of
picked men who could go far on light rations, and Tekbahadur had been chosen to lead it because of his skill
and relentlessness in the jungle. Tekbahadur said he had
served in the Army twelve years now, and during the
Japanese war had been a mortar sergeant in Burma. In
Malaya he had killed three guerrillas so far, all on one occasion; he had been out in front of a patrol and had
walked up on the sentry of a guerrilla camp (a feat needing great stealth); he had stared at the sentry and shot

him, and the patrol had fallen on the camp, killing fifteen altogether and wounding nine. It had been a big action by the standards of Malayan fighting, where weeks or months can be spent in patrolling – in hunting really – before a single enemy is found. Tekbahadur said he was a Magar, a name I learned stood for one of the Nepalese classes or castes the Gurkhas are drawn from.

He and the others talked about Nepal, and it sounded strange and distant, hard to imagine. It was mountainous and poor, they said, so poor that people often died of cold in the winters. It was cut up by hills and rivers, and nearly all travel was on foot; it took fifteen days of walking to reach the orderly's village from the railhead in India, to the south. Most Gurkhas in this regiment came from West Nepal and were Magars or Gurungs, another caste or class there. The state of order was bad in much of West Nepal, and travelers could be attacked by robbers; when Gurkhas went home there on leave they carried a lot of back pay, mainly in gold, and they went in bands armed with their kukris. About the larger politics of Nepal, reputedly an antique country now wracked by modern influence, Tekbahadur and the others had little to say. They said they missed their mountain cold here in Malaya, which steams with tropical heat each day of the year; they missed their sheep and millet, and they weren't satisfied by rice, which made them feel stuffed awhile, then left them empty. The parts of Nepal they came from were high in truth, often ten thousand feet and over –

windswept pastures and snowy peaks — and in the close jungle night it all sounded like another world.

Next morning the patrol left at dawn to cross a wide piece of rubber before tappers appeared. The latex in rubber trees flows best in the morning, so tapping starts early, and the tappers here were said to favor the bandits — they gave them news and kept news from the authorities, through fear or sympathy or both. To hide their movements from tappers' eyes the patrol wore plain sneakers instead of regulation jungle boots, which leave distinctive tracks. We hurried on through the twilight beneath the trees. In half an hour we reached jungle on the other side. We went more slowly then, and soon we stopped for breakfast.

At this halt I got my first real look at the patrol. The men were brown and Mongoloid — that is, they had the long eyes, low noses, high cheekbones and square face lines of the Chinese or Japanese. They looked like Tibetans — Tibet borders Nepal on the north — but they were smaller. They were shoulder high to a tall Englishman. These in the patrol were young, fit and quiet-looking. Tekbahadur seemed different from the rest; he had a more active, histrionic face; was more gay, perhaps sardonic; he smiled often, and partly for effect, it seemed, showing big white teeth. He was lithe and slight, with broad shoulders. When he pointed to our place on the map I saw that his hands were small, fine and square.

Like the others he wore an olive-drab wool shirt, and khaki trousers already wet and stained. The jungle round us was all greens and browns to match. I noted one man leaning against a tree: smooth olive face against smooth olive bark. The light was diffused and gray from the thick leaves overhead, and the men spoke in subdued tones, murmurs, their habit on patrol. Their small figures were gathered here and there among the tall trees, the verticality of the trunks setting off the delicate squareness of their groupings, and of their shoulders, their packs and their faces.

The lieutenant and I sat on a log and watched the radio man string his antenna for a meeting with company headquarters. He had to cut a vine, and he used a British Army machete for this, not his kukri; the lieutenant said most Gurkhas leaned to machetes now for jungle work, as the blades were thinner and harder — could hold a finer edge.

After a wait some tea was brought us in canteen cups; it was hot and very sweet and milky, which I learned is how the Gurkhas like it.

Three monkeys came overhead, jumping noisily from branch to branch, screaming and chattering, not at all afraid.

I walked about and saw the men cooking the rest of breakfast, which came from tins of standard Gurkha rations; the bulk was rice, and on the side were stews of dal — dried peas — and fish. Each can was meant to last one of the soldiers twenty-four hours, but the lieutenant told me they usually shared in pairs; they ate only two meals a day, now and at dusk — nothing but tea at noon. (Sometimes they added bamboo shoots, prickly pears, or edible ferns — things they had learned to find in the jungle.) Most Gurkhas wouldn't eat beef, he said, and each caste had its rules besides this, though for Magars and Gurungs they were much the same.

In time the food was served, and it seemed excellent — the rice well cooked, the dal much spiced, like curry. While we were eating it the radio man made his contact. He talked with the other end in English, but the messages he sent were in Gurkhali, and this, I learned from the lieutenant, was usual. A hybrid language had also sprung up in the Gurkhas, it seemed. Commands were supposed to be in English, but this rule faded a bit — "Load *panch* rounds!" (*panch* meaning five) a Gurkha sergeant might say to his men. The Gurkhali for some quartermaster items showed English origin: jungle boot was *jungli boot;* the fatigue hat worn on patrols was *jungli topi;* ration was *ration.* The plain English alphabet was less often used by Gurkhas than the Army one — "able, baker, charlie," and so on. Many Gurkhas who had long service knew English well, but they rarely spoke it to their officers, who were expected to be fluent in Gurkhali. The lieutenant guiding me, who had not been long with Gurkhas, was studying diligently now, apparently to good effect.

We talked and ate, and the radio man finished his schedule. He had been sending a message about supplies. "They like to be supplied in the field," the lieutenant said, "because they have a better chance of getting new equipment. They like air drops too. The rule is that torn parachutes needn't be turned back in, and somehow they all get torn in the jungle." Gurkhas, it seemed, had much in common with other troops.

Later that morning, some distance from our breakfast place, we reached a clearing with tall grass, and pink-flowered shrubs the height of alders. It was near the edge of rubber, and I guessed it had been used by Chinese squatters; two years ago Malaya had squatters in the hundreds of thousands, but most have since been gathered in camps because they fed the bandits. Something had crossed the clearing in the grass, and the track caught the eye of Tekbahadur, who all the time had been alert and restless. He took three men and started out to follow it, while we others settled down. The lieutenant said the track seemed new, as the grass hadn't stood up in it yet; it was broad as if trodden by human feet instead of the wild pigs that abound in Malaya; and it might lead out to a bandit camp from the plantation, whose laborers were surely supplying food. Patrols often found camps that way, he said, and when they did the Gurkha scouts could nearly always get close without detection.

From what I saw and heard then, and from later inquiry, I gathered that the jungle craft of Gurkhas isn't perfect. Most Gurkha units keep patrol dogs to sniff out ambushes; and some, though not all, use Dyak trackers from Borneo, real jungle men who can see traces where all looks undisturbed to others. But the Gurkha edge on British troops is huge, as had strikingly been shown a while earlier by another battalion, the First of the Tenth Gurkha Rifles, in the Malayan state of Pahang, to which it had just been moved. Hardly was the move finished before a patrol of these Gurkhas, four or five of them, had walked straight into a famous bandit of the region, Manap Jepun, and shot him dead. Manap was noted for his cunning, and it was thought he had often been approached this way by British patrols and had heard them and hidden. But the Gurkhas had come on him like a silent breeze, and that had been that. Many people cited this instance to me as typical.

We waited in the clearing, and before long the men came back, and I noted we could hear them rustling awhile in the coarse grass. They had found that humans hadn't used the track for some time, Tekbahadur said; the only late travelers had been pigs. He rolled his eyes dramatically, and put two fingers of each hand forward like cloven pig feet, and moved the hands as if walking.

We went on through different kinds of country after that. We started to cross an expanse where the smaller jungle trees had been felled and the larger ones poisoned and left to die, while rubber seedlings had been planted. But the front of the patrol saw someone ahead, and Tekbahadur went to investigate. It was naggingly hot while we waited in the sun; the big poisoned trees looked like ghosts, though some had parasite plants still living high up in them, green and healthy. Tekbahadur came back, his face shining in sweat, and held up a finger; there was only one man ahead, he said, an old one, felling trees. Even so we detoured, trusting no one.

We passed through tall virgin jungle, thick second-growth jungle, and clearings. In the virgin jungle it was cool when we halted. When moving, the patrol kept strung out in formation — three men in front, a command group, a Bren gun, and so on. Tekbahadur ranged about ceaselessly. The day wore on. By afternoon the mood had slackened. The lieutenant said the hours were always felt on these patrols; there was a sense of danger in the morning that burned off by midday.

Around midafternoon we crossed a swamp, dry now in the season of light rains; it was a bandit hangout but we found nothing; and after that the lieutenant and I pulled out to join some transport waiting for us. The men kept on patrolling cheerfully.

Back at battalion headquarters I tried, by questioning the officers and reading things they showed me, to learn a little of the Gurkha castes or classes. This took some time and I pursued it on and off; what I found was complicated, and I shall note only a fraction of it here.

To begin with, the name Gurkha as used in the British Army means a man from any of the several Nepalese warrior castes.

The Second Gurkha Rifles, like the Sixth, is drawn from West Nepal, and made up chiefly of Magars and Gurungs.

The Seventh and Tenth, the other two British regiments, are from East Nepal and made up chiefly of castes called Rais and Limbus. Rais and Lumbus are deemed more flighty — and perhaps more keen and enterprising — than Magars and Gurungs.

There are some nonfighting (and lower) Nepalese castes that the Army has uses for, including the Sarkhis (shoemakers), the Kamis or Lohars (blacksmiths) and the Damais (tailors). These are recruited, but not to bear arms. A few of each were serving at the 2/6 headquarters, and I saw them in their shops; they looked different from the actual Gurkhas, their faces tending to be Indian and aquiline rather than Mongoloid.

There are many oddities of caste besides those noted above, but they are of concern mainly in recruiting. In the day-to-day life of troops, it seems, food is the chief problem. As a rule, if a Gurkha eats food cooked by anyone lower in caste, or eats in company with those of the menial castes, he loses caste himself — becomes *pani band*, it is called — and stays that way till he goes through a purifying ritual.

No Gurkha will eat of female goats or sheep. I saw a billy goat wandering round the headquarters one afternoon, and asked an officer who owned it. It was in the ration, he said; it had been issued on the hoof so the troops could be sure what they were getting. There had been talk, he said, of sending a party of Gurkhas to Australia, a big Army meat source, to guarantee the sex of mutton packed there, but nothing had yet come of this.

By tradition Gurungs and Magars have opposite types of "cross-cousin marriages." A Gurung may marry the daughter of his father's sister. A Magar may not, but may marry the daughter of his mother's brother. Cross-cousin marriages are in the older style, though, and are being dropped nowadays.

The Gurungs retain a good deal of Buddhism, which was once their main religion (as it is still that of their neighbors the Tibetans), but the Magars have come more fully under Hinduism. Hinduism was brought to Nepal only a few centuries ago, by fugitives from the Muslim conquest of India. Since then it has spread its influence through all but the higher mountain regions, and the barriers of caste have grown with the spreading, caste being a Hindu idea. Today Nepal is looked on as a Hindu country.

The Bhagavad Gita, the great Hindu gospel, is a dialogue between the divine Krishna and the warrior Arjuna, and much of it deals with fighting-caste obligations. The dialogue takes place on the eve of a battle from which Arjuna recoils because he sees only misery and bloodshed in it for all. Krishna tells him to stand up and fight, saying death is unimportant, not worth grieving over, and Arjuna will sin if he turns from his role. It is a moving passage; it had struck me as the most heartening thing possible for those engaging in warfare; and I wondered whether it, and the beliefs connected with it, had much to do with the Gurkhas' penchant for arms. I asked

some of the British officers about this, and they didn't
think much of the idea (though there must be depths of
Gurkha thought they do not know). They believed
pay was nearly the whole thing, and they made a good
case for this, Nepal being so poor a country and the
Gurkhas such poor hill people. Gurkha soldiers spend
their prime in the Army, and the money they have to
show for it softens their old age or that of their parents.
(The money isn't saved spontaneously, the officers said
in passing, but is withheld by the Army — in an effort, no
doubt, to make the system a success, and popular at
home.)

I stayed in the battalion officers mess a couple of days.
It was a frame building on a high knoll that caught the
breeze. All round us, far to the distance, lay flatlands in
rubber and jungle, pierced now and then by solitary
hills in jungle too, good bandit havens. Other buildings
— offices, shops, cookhouses, quarters for soldiers and
families — clung on the knoll's sides and round its base;
this was the battalion's home; it had no other. In the mess
were cups, medals, pictures of high Nepalese, prints of
game birds and of an 1819 "Gorkah" soldier, and paintings of two men from Gurkha units — a Gurkha and an
Englishman — who had won the VC in Burma. The officers were kind and hospitable. British officers of Gurkhas are somewhat an elite; besides being based in a far
country — expatriated — they are more vulnerable in battle than their fellows, being more easily distinguished by
snipers from their troops; in the past they have been dis-

couraged from marriage, a state distracting to a soldier, as Kipling noted, though the rules are slackening now; they get extra pay, some of it for learning Gurkhali; and in general they strike one as having a high morale and a liking for their men beyond the usual.

I asked them what the Gurkhas' strong points were. Amenability to discipline, I was told; toughness, enthusiasm; patience; loyalty to their officers. Gurkhas were like Cockneys in some ways, a major said, but not in discipline; if a Gurkha were sent up the wrong hill he could be called down and sent up the right one and would go gladly; few other troops would do that. Another major thought it important that Gurkhas were countrymen, mountain men; these always made good soldiers. They were not natural shots, it was said, but could be taught. They were poor at technical things — at using complex gear — but good at straight infantry work, and above all in rough country; a major who had led a Gurkha battalion in Italy said it wound up making most of its brigade's advances in the mountains there. On patrol Gurkhas moved about well, but could report only sketchily when they came back.

They could scarcely be called a disciplinary problem at all, I gathered; they were pleasant and easy; they liked rum and liked women to a fair degree, but they didn't get in trouble. Much of their good behavior could be laid, the officers thought, to the fact they were volunteers; and they could also drop quietly out, if unhappy, on a trip home for leave; this might be desertion, but it was overlooked — had to be, as Nepal was out of reach. "There's none of this sordid business of chasing deserters up," a major said.

Some officers said the Gurkhas could find their way unaided from point to point in the jungle, a feat beyond most Westerners. One morning I saw a class being taught compass work by a Scottish sergeant (the Gurkhas have a few British other ranks — noncoms — with them as teachers and technicians). I asked how they took to the compass. "Oh, they're interested in its mechanics," the sergeant said, "but they don't need it." He pointed to his beret. "They've got one in their head." I was with a captain then, and he told me of a Gurkha who had vanished in the Burma jungle for several days, and after returning had shown his superior, on the map, the route he had followed; on second glance the map had turned out to be of the London Underground; or so the story went.

I learned later, by the way, that British other ranks who serve with Gurkhas often re-enlist. This is against the trend, as under National Service — conscription — most British soldiers stay in the Army no longer than they have to. But British sergeants here hung out at the Gurkha sergeants' mess, and got to like it, and in the end they wanted more.

The battalion commander, a lieutenant colonel, thought that a Gurkha would hold a salute while being run down by a truck. He had much regard for their patience and stamina, and he told about an eight-man

patrol from the battalion that had just gone five days in
the jungle without food; they had been told to go to a
stream that existed, it turned out, only on the map; of
course they hadn't found it, and meanwhile their radio
had failed, but they had decided on their own to keep
on going; they had done this, had turned back two days
later, and in time had come out quietly at the starting
place. They hadn't seemed too proud of the performance, which would have been a prodigy if done by
Westerners.

The colonel thought highly of their courage too; he
thought they would face anything if trained or led properly. The other officers seemed to feel as he did, some
laying the courage to simplicity. "They are not imaginative," one said, "and therefore not apprehensive." From
what I learned at the battalion I believe most stories of
Gurkha feats in Burma or North Africa may be myths.
But it seemed true that in one case anyway two companies of Gurkhas had wiped out one of Japanese with
kukris alone. This showed what they could do.

I was told the Gurkhas were "not good at games, but
frightfully keen," and the keenness showed in the late
afternoons on playing fields by the knoll's foot. There
were two fields there for soccer and one for volleyball,
a game newly popular with Gurkhas, and at the due hour
their green turf was overrun by a throng of smallish
brown bodies, thickset and stripped to the waist, bouncing zestfully, rushing together and apart, high spirited
and good natured too, active despite the heat. I was told

Gurkhas like hunting, fishing, games, gambling, singing, dancing and drinking. To a large degree, it seemed, their culture was that of ordinary camp or barracks life. Apart from seeing Indian movies now and then they had few pursuits one might call intellectual. The regiment had bagpipes — there is some Scotch influence on Gurkha units — but for private music the men used only a long small drum, the size of a stove log, each end giving out a different note. A platoon could stay happy with one for evenings at a time, a major told me — beating it and chanting. Sometimes, he added, the Gurkhas staged a nautch dance too, a Nepalese form, and he thought they might show me one before I left.

In my stay I sometimes walked near the family lines, the quarters of Gurkha wives and children. A fourth of the married men had families with them now, a captain told me; they took turns; when these went on leave their families would stay in Nepal, while others came to Malaya; it was hoped more could be brought on soon, and the lines expanded. The lines were in frame buildings on the hillside and in wall tents on the flat. The officers seemed unhappy about the latter, and thought the Gurkha women did well to put up with them, and keep them as clean as they did. Often when you glanced into a tent you saw feminine touches there: a colored cloth laid on a table, some flowers in a vase. Plants flourished round the lines: flowers, corn, beans, papayas, tapioca; Gurkhas had green thumbs, the colonel said. The women, like the men, were straight and rather broad, and they wore straight-hanging pigtails that set this off. They wore bodices that ran to solid colors — rose, black and canary yellow were some I noted — with long full skirts wound round their hips in folds; the skirt with the black bodice was in lilac. They seemed very Himalayan. They wore earrings and nose jewelry of gold — often elaborate and often set with stones. They could be seen watering flowers, or sitting with children in the afternoon, or eating at nightfall with their husbands on the floor. They looked quiet, domestic, classical.

The children too wore jewelry. The battalion had a school for the smaller ones, and with the colonel I looked in the door one day. A half dozen pupils stood there, somewhat over knee high, before a blackboard on which was chalked the English alphabet; a little boy, in shirt and shorts and with a golden nose ring, pointed to the letters and sang them out while the others echoed him in chorus.

The birth rate in the lines was high, I gathered, and a baby's arrival brought eleven days' rejoicing to its family; but its father couldn't join in the first ten of these; he had to keep apart then, and at the end be put through cleansing rites before coming back to circulation. The rites were handled by the battalion priest, a remote personage, Nepalese, whom I didn't meet; I gathered his duties were mainly ceremonial, not social and educational like a Western chaplain's, though I am not sure of this.

During my stay I kept wondering about Nepal, but it
was still dim to me when I left. It was clearly a poor,
overpeopled country whose chief export was men — for
years Nepalese gangs had worked in Burma and the As-
sam tea estates, and here and there — in Singapore, for
instance — Gurkhas served as policemen. Most proceeds
of the export went home in gold. Besides the jewelry on
their wives and children — always treated as negotiable
in Asia — Gurkhas bought bullion with their pay before
each leave. And they bought commodities like cloth and
cigarettes. Then they vanished toward their mountains.

The night before I went away a nautch was staged in
the Gurkha officers' mess. It was impromptu and not to
be compared, I was told, with the big battalion-size
nautches put on now and then, especially at the time of
Dashera, the chief Gurkha festival (on a morning of
which young buffaloes and other animals are beheaded
with kukris, preferably in one stroke each). Now our
time was short — just a while before dinner — and the
room in the Gurkha officers' mess was narrow, allowing
but half a dozen dancers. I sat next the chief clerk, a
Gurkha schooled in India who spoke good English. Both
men's and women's parts were danced by soldiers —
married Nepalese women don't appear this way, I gathered, and of course there were no girls. The music was
slow, to the beat of small long drums, and many people
chanted. It sounded like Tibetan singing I had heard.
The dancers came forward and fell back, crouching, ris-

ing, whirling, very graceful. The "girls" wore bodices, long skirts and veils in bright aniline colors — reds, greens, yellows — and in their headbands they had cheap jewelry, among it imitation coral. They were dancing to religious and love songs both, the chief clerk said. In some the words were improvised; the Gurkhas did this often; they had made up a whole saga of their deeds in Italy. The rhythm quickened and intensified. The drums beat harder, more people sang, the dancers whirled more catchingly. It warmed and gripped us and I felt torn when we rose to leave. Big nautches, I was told, make a real night of it — dancing till nearly dawn; much rum consumed; much hospitality: a brimming dose of Gurkha openhandedness.

Next morning I left the battalion in convoy with an ambulance taking a wounded Gurkha down to Singapore. The Gurkha had been shot through the jaw but didn't seem to mind. "He's all right," a medical sergeant said when seeing us off. "The worse the wound the better they are — that's the way with these Gurkhas." I rode in a scout car guarding the ambulance; on that road no army vehicle might go alone. The driver was a British sergeant, one of those who had served with Gurkhas and re-enlisted to serve again. He was close mouthed though pleasant. I asked him what he thought of Gurkhas. "They're good blokes," he said; and later he said it again in answer to more questioning; and it was all he said on the subject in our three hours' drive. And as we went along I felt it was all he needed to say.

Old Man River

THE BIGGEST dam now under construction in the world, so far as Westerners know, is at Bhakra, India, in the foothills of the Himalayas. It is in a class with the biggest American dams and is far greater than any yet built in Asia, barring something unknown to us on the Ob, the Yenisei or another Siberian river. Its building is mainly the responsibility of Harvey Slocum, an American construction man who seems to have been created on the grand scale himself. Slocum is an original thinker and a nonstop talker who often expresses himself in four-letter words. He wastes little time on modesty, and he has no doubts about the greatness of his task at Bhakra. "I am not exaggerating a bit if I tell you this is the toughest job of all time," he said to me recently at the dam site. I had gone to spend a week end with him and get some notion of what he and Bhakra were like. While there I stayed in a small stucco house, a few miles from the dam, where Slocum lives as a virtual hermit, with one Indian servant to wait on him and with no intimate friends. He told me he practiced this solitude on purpose, and had done the same in America, where he had bossed some big jobs before coming to India. "I don't have friends," he said, "and I don't play favorites. I don't invite people to my house. You *can't* have friends. One of these jobs is a battle; you are fighting nature. Now the only friend General Grant had was his whiskey bottle; he confided in that, I understand. . . ." This reminded Slocum of how a friend of his, an old-time contractor, had replied many years ago to some criticism of Slocum's drinking (a habit he had gone in for diligently then, but has since discarded). "This old contractor said: 'You know how I feel about Harvey Slocum. I feel as Lincoln said about Grant, that he wished all the other generals would drink the same brand of whiskey.' " Slocum paused a moment. "That contractor also paid me the highest compliment I've ever been paid in my life," he went on, "and I've never forgotten it. He said: 'Harvey Slocum is the only intrinsically honest man I have ever known.' "

Discourses like this, which Slocum would sometimes keep up for long periods, did not pall on me during my visit. They may seem egotistical in print, but when spoken they had a thoughtfulness or objectivity that was the reverse of this. They were also delivered with a verve like that of W. C. Fields. To me they were welcome contributions to the knowledge I sought: an understanding of Slocum himself. Nor did the reference to Grant in this speech — or at least to Civil War generals — seem inappropriate. Slocum told me that his father had been a first cousin of General Sherman's; and Slocum himself looked like Sherman, especially above the mouth; he had the same prominent nose, thoughtful eyes, and high, rather narrow brow. He was sixty-eight years old, he told me, and his hair was gray (it was also slicked down and receding). He had a fine, lean face, with deep lines from the nose to the corners of the mouth, and the skin was scarred from a severe burning of years ago. His mouth was strong, curly and thin lipped. The skin on his hands seemed almost corrugated with scars from the same burning, and his handshake was very firm. He was of medium height, straight as a ramrod, and his head was set on well. He seemed to have the quality one might expect in Sherman, and as I got to know him I felt he had a drasticness of mind that must be like Sherman's too — I could well imagine him, for example, stating that war was hell and then fighting a war with no holds barred.

In the daytime I drove round the dam site a good deal with Slocum. The dam is being built in a narrow gorge of the Siwalik Range, an outwork of the Himalayas. This range stands up straight like a wall, many hundreds of feet high, and the river in question, the Sutlej, had simply cut a gap through it. The dam, whose foundations were now being poured, was supposed to plug the gap, or gorge, and make a reservoir behind it by filling up an expanse of the valley there, between the Siwalik Range and the Himalayas proper. The gorge was like a narrow

V, several hundreds of feet high, and men and machines were working at various levels on both of its sides, as well as in its bottom. A continuous supply of materials was being brought to them, from lower down the Sutlej, by trucks, by a small railway, and by a four-mile-long conveyor belt. Also at different levels on the gorge's side a number of big installations had been fixed, such as cranes, concrete-mixing plants, workshops, gravel sorters and a clump of administration buildings. It was an elaborate layout in three dimensions. "The tremendous complexity of the God-damn thing!" Slocum would declare cheerfully as we drove into sight of it, coming from his house. The complexity was all linked together by gravel roads, which zigzagged up and down the gorge's sides, sometimes passing through tunnels. We drove up and down these in Slocum's car, a 1951 Oldsmobile coupé, yellow with a black top, which he had used on his last previous job in the States. Slocum wore dark glasses, a khaki hat, khaki trousers and a khaki shirt open at the neck. He also carried a pad and pencil, and he would often jot down notes when we were not in motion — he always drove the car himself. Sometimes we would pull up at a key spot by the dam site, and certain of Slocum's lieutenants — Indian, American or both — would be waiting there for a conference, or, more exactly, a receiving of orders; Slocum did most of the talking at these sessions; he knew what he wanted and he would impart this, firmly and directly. Now and then he would listen to someone else, but like other creative people I have

known he really seemed absorbed in his own vision of
the job, and interested mainly in expressing this. He also
seemed rather military, like a strict general talking to
subordinates. Once I attended a meeting in his office,
where a half dozen of his Indian and American helpers
were present, and he did most of the talking there too.
He sat straight in his chair and laid the program down
with gusto, often pointing a finger at one of his listeners.
After that meeting I talked briefly with one of the
American assistants, who seemed to have an affection
for Slocum. "He likes to leave the impression of being a
mighty hard man," this assistant said, "but he's really
not. He's being hard to make 'em do the things they
should do, but wouldn't do otherwise. As long as you're
trying, no matter whether you know the job or not, he'll
help you. But if you're not trying he'll keep on riding
you." This assistant thought that planning was Slocum's
long suit. "On the planning the old man has done a first-
class job," he said. "There isn't anyone better than he at
that."

I got the impression, while driving round with Slocum,
that he was thinking all the time – that he had a picture
in his mind of the dam when finished, and of all the steps
to be taken in the meanwhile, and that he kept referring
mentally to this picture, and changing it if need be, as he
looked the scene over. The question of timing occupied
him a lot. Slocum said that with luck the dam might be
finished in 1962. Meanwhile many things had to be done,
each in its own time. While I was there, for instance, an

American specialist arrived to supervise the building of the penstocks — the giant steel tubes that would run down through the dam, bringing water to the turbines at its base. These would not be installed for three more years, but their construction had to begin now — indeed Slocum complained that the work was getting off to a slow start because the steel involved, which had been ordered in Japan, had been late in arriving. Again, in 1958 the reservoir would start filling, according to Slocum's plan, and many things — including a couple of workmen's villages — had to be moved before that happened. Meanwhile there would be seasonal floods each year — from the melting snows in spring and the monsoons in summer — that had to be allowed for. Finally there was the problem of winding up the job, to be thought of already. Most of the dam's excavation and preliminary work had been done now, Slocum explained, and the main task ahead was the mixing and placing of concrete. Therefore he kept telling his staff to get rid of needlessly varied equipment — to simplify and standardize, and to come out at the end with as little in the warehouses as possible. The equipment was varied because Bhakra had had to make many things that in other countries would simply be bought. "No other construction job in the world has this kind of a layout," Slocum said once. "You make everything yourself except for growing the trees." The Bhakra empire was rather like an island, in fact, amid the primitive Indian economy. Slocum told me he had the only truck-trailer equipment in India, the only hopper-bottom cement cars in India, and the only shop in India that could retread the big tires used by bulldozers and other construction gear. These things had more than paid for themselves, he said. The retreading shop, for instance, had made it unnecessary to buy extra tires so that some could always be working while others were off on months-long trips to a distant industrial center. Slocum had had difficulty in persuading the Indians, who are not used to lavishness with machinery, that his approach was sound, but he felt he had succeeded on the whole. He had even put in diesel-electric engines on the dam's railway and had proved these to be a saving. Down on the flatland below the foothills, in a basing area called Nangal, he had a big yard with shops, railway sidings and endless stacks of supplies, which he claimed was the best materials-handling yard in India. The shops were adorned with signs in English, saying things like SAFETY IS FREE — USE IT GENEROUSLY; NEVER PUT OFF TILL TOMORROW WHAT YOU CAN DO TODAY; and BEAUTY OF THE HOUSE IS ORDER. This last motto was significant. Slocum confessed to being a martinet about housekeeping, as he called it, and everywhere at the dam site materials awaiting use — even big things like girders — were stacked as neatly as pins. "I've been accused by many people of being a perfectionist," Slocum told me. "And they are right." He added that neatness cut his accident rate down sharply.

He said he kept inventing devices on the job, or improving them. The endless conveyor belts, which hauled gravel to the dam from farther down the Sutlej, had electrical attachments to stop them if anything went wrong. Slocum said he had invented these, and that they were generally known as "Slocum-tronics." He had worked out a special combination of AC and DC current for his cranes, and special pulley rigs for them, so their cables wouldn't twist; and he had air-conditioned their control cabs and put swivel chairs in these, so the operators would be alert on the job. He had built a huge concrete-mixing plant, on the scale of a grain elevator, whose operations were almost wholly automatic; and he had a special plant for cooling down the gravel before it was mixed — this was the best way, he said, of countering the fact that cement heats troublesomely as it sets. He didn't say he had invented all these things, but he had at least improved them as he went about on the job, thinking. He had also made changes in the dam's design, though this was not his province — he was not a graduate engineer, and engineering matters were supposed to be under a "consulting board" of men, both Indian and American, who were. Slocum called it his "insulting board." Slocum was a member of the board too, but I gathered that he had had brushes with it about such matters as the rock structure at the dam site and how it should be dealt with, and that he had come out successfully on the whole. "On a job like this you've got to be a specialist in everything," he told me once. "You subcontract nothing, and that's what I like. I like to be doing it all myself. I like the challenge." On more than one occasion in the States, Slocum also told me, he had refused to boss construction jobs for certain contracting firms unless the firms' heads would promise to stay in their New York offices and not come near the actual sites. The latter had balked at these tyrannical conditions, but Slocum had held firm too, and the deals had not come off.

The monsoons at Bhakra were a great problem, I gathered, because during them it rained and rained, and the hillsides might get soggy and start moving. Slocum habitually made three trips to America each year, but he was never away from Bhakra in the monsoon season. In the year before my visit the rains had been unusually heavy — the worst in one hundred years, it was generally said — and slides had begun all over the place. Apparently Slocum had directed the operations against them rather as a military commander would direct field operations. "When the countryside is moving you have to decide instantly on changes," he told me. "You can't be away, and you can't hold consultations." We were driving along near the dam site, and Slocum showed me where he had put in new roads and drainage systems at the height of last year's emergency. He was wagging a finger and sounding more like W. C. Fields than ever. "Napoleon, Eisenhower, Alexander the Great," he said with resonance, "all the great generals had the faculty of looking at the God-damn thing and saying 'Do this.' They could talk things over before the battle, but not during it." While at Bhakra I gathered that the faculty of saying "Do this" was among Slocum's main contributions to the job. Work had begun on the dam some

years before he had been hired, but it had bogged down
for lack of anyone with the experience and confidence to
go lightheartedly ahead with the roads, tunnels and other
big side projects that were necessary, even though they
would not show in the final result. Indian (and European) engineers previously on the job had not come to
grips with these problems, but Slocum had tackled them
straight off on his arrival. "You had to recognize what
you had to do, and the magnitude of the thing," he explained to me, "and then go ahead and do it in a big
way. That's what none of these other fellows could
realize. All these roads and all that had to be thought out
at the beginning, not at the end." And the roads at Bhakra
were a major construction job in themselves.

While staying with Slocum I learned something of
his early life. His father, General Sherman's cousin, was
born in 1832 and must have been rather like Slocum
himself. He was a New Englander and good at building
things, and he traveled down South while a young man
and eventually out to California. Slocum says his father
was a natural executive, and he thinks that he himself
inherited this quality — as did an older sister of his who
ran a business office in California till she retired a while
ago, at the age of seventy. Slocum's maternal grand-
mother was also a natural executive, he says. His mother
was a freethinker, and something of a mystic or spiritual-
ist, who "got very much enamored of numbers and
colors and all that sort of thing." She accepted life gen-

erously, saying she got some kind of benefit from every experience, and she was a great believer in her son Harvey. Slocum was often criticized in his youth for wild behavior. "You leave Harvey alone," his mother used to say at such times. "He'll come out all right." The Slocums were poor when Harvey was a boy, and he went to work at the age of thirteen — he went to San Francisco, he says, and got a job as messenger boy in the Barbary Coast, associating there with prostitutes, gamblers and "the worst God-damn riffraff in the world." He says this life might have ruined him if he had stayed in it long, and it has left him with a distrust of other men. "I don't trust men," he says. "I've known too many of them. But I trust some women. I trust my wife absolutely." His wife, whose name is Helen, lives in California and doesn't come with him to India — indeed one can hardly imagine what she would do in the hermitlike, work-absorbed atmosphere at Bhakra.

Slocum got out of the Barbary Coast in his teens, he says, by learning the cabinetmaker's trade. Then he drifted into structural ironwork, and into heavy construction generally, and by thirty he was in dam building. "I naturally became the boss on all jobs," he says, "even unfamiliar ones, because I liked to work and am naturally smart. I was a natural boss, a natural executive." He must also have been tough. It was during this period that he got his burn scars, from a virtual explosion on a construction job (the scars cover much of his body, he says, as well as his face and hands). He was taken to the hospital and given emergency treatment, though without much hope it would pull him through. The next morning the doctor came to see him and the following dialogue took place, according to Slocum:

DOCTOR: So you're still here?

SLOCUM: Where the hell did you think I was going to be?

DOCTOR: I was sure you'd be dead.

A few days later the doctor ordered Slocum's daily bath omitted. Slocum asked why and was told he was thought too weak to stand it. He then asked if not taking the bath would guarantee his survival, and when told it wouldn't he said he would take it anyway, as he would just as soon die in the tub as in bed. Eventually he recovered. It took him a long time to regain the use of his hands and legs, but he did this too; and he continued upward in the building trade. He soon reached a point where he had to deal with paper work, though he had never gone beyond the eighth grade. He was naturally good at reading blueprints, he says, but was poor at figures. "I didn't have the bookkeeper type of mind," he explains. "I thought the fellow who figured out the costs must have come from Mars. But I made up my mind to find out how they did it. I began making my own estimates. I would get some plans — say from the city government — and make an estimate on the job, and then go and see a contractor. I would show it to him and listen to his comments. 'Where is the insurance?' he would ask. 'Where is the overhead?' And in that way I learned what was supposed to go into the damn thing. Then I evolved a system of my own. I do it by visualizing everything I am going to need and then writing it down. And any contractor in the United States would rather have a Slocum estimate than someone else's."

Slocum kept on rising till he became the construction boss of Grand Coulee, the biggest dam ever built. Later he bossed the construction of Friant Dam in California and Bull Shoals Dam in Arkansas, two other big ones. During the war he worked on military projects like the Alcan Highway. He is sometimes called "the best dam man in the world," and last winter he was given the annual nonmember award of the Moles — a New York association of tunnel builders and heavy-construction men — as well as an award of the Beavers, a Los Angeles group that is the Moles' West Coast counterpart. The Moles award — which in earlier years has gone to Herbert Hoover, Robert Moses and General Brehon B. Somervell, among others — is said to be highly regarded, and Slocum doesn't conceal his pleasure at getting it. He has received a good volume of congratulatory mail about it, from both Indians and Americans, the latter including Jim Farley and Vice-President Nixon. He confesses to liking the "dignity" of such recognition. He was also pleased by his election, in 1943, to the Bohemian Club in San Francisco. He is apparently becoming an elder statesman of the building community. When passing through New Delhi he nearly always pays a long call on Pandit Nehru. He says he has made fourteen trips round the world now (all by Pan American Airways), without counting lesser trips like a recent one to Spain, where he surveyed some dam possibilities for certain Spanish power companies. To some extent he is taking on the role of polished globetrotter along with that of roughneck dam builder. The two seem to mix all right. The rough talk of dam builders is a rather superficial convention, I gathered while at Bhakra, which can be laid aside easily by a thoughtful man. And Slocum would always be Slocum anyway, one feels, no matter what part he was theoretically playing.

The Indian authorities first got in touch with Slocum about Bhakra in 1945, when the dam was still little more than a dream. Nothing came of this meeting, or of subsequent ones in 1948 and 1949. In 1950 an Indian delegation got him to come and look at the site, following which he wrote them a letter giving his views on a suitable contract. He gave them ninety days to act on this, and then extended the time by thirty more days, but they couldn't make up their minds, and Slocum told them to forget it. He seems to have been keen on the job at first, but to have cooled off by this time — some choice spots in America were open to him, for one thing. The Indians, on the other hand, seem to have been growing more eager all the time. The dam meant a lot to them — more than any other project envisaged in their new independence — and it was obviously not going to get built by itself. So in the fall of 1951 a delegation approached

Slocum again. He was truly reluctant by now, but agreed to have his lawyer outline a contract. The terms were very favorable to Slocum, and the lawyer assured him that no individual, much less a government, would sign such an instrument. Nevertheless the Indians did sign it, and Slocum felt bound to sign in return. Under the contract he is required to do three things only — to design a construction plant for the dam; to hire men if instructed to do so in writing; and to purchase equipment, also if instructed in writing. In addition the Indian authorities may consult him at any time he is in their country, though his total sojourn there need not exceed four months each year. Slocum's pay is not public knowledge, but it is generally thought to approach a hundred thousand dollars a year and to be the best salary in India excepting the allowances of a few maharajahs. For him the Indian Government also keeps a six-figure bank account in America, which he draws on for his expenses — he is the sole judge of what these shall include — and which India replenishes promptly. It sounds like a wastrel's dream of a contract — all in Slocum's favor — but actually it seems to be a good bargain for India. In effect it makes Slocum stake his whole personality on Bhakra. "When I signed it," he says, "I incurred the only obligation that's worth a damn, anywhere in the world, an obligation to myself." There seems to be no doubt of Slocum's devotion to Bhakra, and he says he will see the job through unless he dies on it.

*   *   *

There is a wooden sign outside the post office that serves the Bhakra-Nangal Project, as it is officially called, and this sign bears the following legend:

BHAKRA SYMBOL OF INDIA'S PROGRESS

Bhakra-Nangal Project is something tremendous, something stupendous and something which shakes you up when you see it. Bhakra today is the symbol of India's progress. The gigantic work they had undertaken at Bhakra symbolized the people's faith & determination to march ahead.

JAWAHAR LAL NEHRU

It does seem that Indians, from Nehru down, sense an identity between Bhakra's fortunes and those of their new country. They show Bhakra off to foreigners in this spirit too. The state guests visiting India in recent winters have usually been taken to Bhakra right after being feted at New Delhi, the capital; and a routine for welcoming them has grown up there. In driving round the Bhakra environs with Slocum I saw wooden skeletons of festive arches standing over the road at various points. Slocum said these had been appropriately decked out a few days earlier for the Shah of Persia, the most recent state guest, and would probably soon be decked out afresh for someone else. And arches might be added or subtracted the next time too. "It's all according to how big a shot they are how many arches are put up," he explained. Indian tourists also visit Bhakra in volume, and the place seems to have a strong emotional impact on them. The idea of dams is significant in India anyway, and in certain other old countries of Asia, because the civilizations of these places grew up round irrigation in remote antiquity (and have hence been called "hydraulic" civilizations by some scholars). The plain below Bhakra probably had an irrigation system long before the Christian Era, and this has been improved or restored at various times since then — notably by the British during their rule. The dams of these earlier periods, however, were mere *diversion* dams as a rule — ones that would block the water from its normal course and shunt it into a canal, through which it would keep flowing to another locality, coming to rest only on the soil it was meant to water. Bhakra adds a new dimension to this concept because it is a *storage* dam, designed to hold back water in the flood seasons and release it in the dry ones — to alter the river's flow in time, that is, as well as in space. Big storage dams are a new thing in India, and they can probably add much scope to the irrigation there. Bhakra will bring more than six and a half million new acres into cultivation, I was told by an Indian engineer whom I talked with during my visit. It will also permit some new refinements because of the new seasonal control it affords — its water can be released at strategic moments in the life cycles of the various crops that grow in that region, and this will mean more added fertility than the mere added volume of water suggests. There will also be a good power output at Bhakra — approaching a million kilowatts at times — and this will help new industries to start, both at the dam site and far away. A fertilizer plant is already contemplated in the Bhakra neighborhood, and Slocum predicts that all sorts of industries, now undreamed of, will grow up there. Development on this scale is a new thing for India, as for Asia generally. India is a poor country, but in Bhakra she should have a modern public asset comparable to the best ones of rich countries like America.

Comparing dams is not an enthralling pursuit, but it does yield some knowledge. Bhakra is in a class with the three biggest American dams, namely Grand Coulee, Hoover and Shasta. In volume of concrete used it is ahead of Hoover, but behind Shasta and Grand Coulee. In storage capacity, and power-generating capacity, it is ahead of Shasta, but behind Grand Coulee and Hoover. In height its rank isn't sure yet, because of an argument between Slocum and his "insulting board," but he says it will definitely be over seven hundred feet, and will therefore be in competition with Hoover for first place (the latter's height is seven hundred and twenty-six feet). I was given these comparisons by Slocum, who cited the figures concerned from memory. He said that so far as he knew there was nothing else in a class with these four dams. The famous Russian dams, he said, could not compare in height or in volume of concrete, though they might do so in power or storage capacity. Some of the earth dams in the Missouri Valley, such as Fort Peck, might rank near the top in storage capacity too, but not in anything else. Slocum said a dam higher than the four giants was being planned in Switzerland, but it would be built in stages, over a long period. The Aswan High Dam in Egypt would be a big one too, if it got built. Otherwise he knew of nothing approaching Bhakra and its three American compeers.

Once during my visit I tore myself away and went to have a look at the dam site by myself. I went up to the highest road on one side of the gorge, just above where the top of the dam was scheduled to be. From there the gorge was like a deep pit below me, more than seven hundred feet down. Across it, on the far side, stood a huge wall of gray and brown rock, which had been exposed by excavations, and to which the other side of the dam would be anchored. Its face looked brittle and fragmented, with an underlying pattern of layers — stratifications — that had once been horizontal but were now almost vertical, thanks to some past folding action. It was the uptilting of these layers that had made the Siwalik Range. The top of the wall facing me was crowned by a green fuzz of vegetation — pines, grass, and so forth — and a road cut across the bottom of this green, at about the same level as my own perch. A loaded mule train was crawling along it now, headed back into the mountains. Lower down, the raw facing wall was cut across by half a dozen shallow, slanting terraces, which were roads that Slocum had built for use in the construction process. Hundreds of feet below me, near the bottom of the far wall, some excavation was being done. There was a big pile of brown dusty earth there, looking like malted-milk powder, and on it four bulldozers, seeming like insects to me, were at work. There were perhaps a hundred men, much tinier, down there too; they were hardly distinguishable except for their white tin helmets. Between them and me, supported on trestles in the middle of the gorge, four aluminum-painted cranes were working — lifting dirt from the excavation or placing concrete in the dam's foundations. The cranes looked like toys to me, though I knew their booms were more than a hundred and fifty feet long. A general murmur rose from the pit. Its components were the noises of diesel engines, of pneumatic drills, of girders clanking and even of sirens screaming. But the mixture was just a hum when I didn't analyze it. And it was drowned out, from time to time, by gusts of wind that came through the pass high up, where I was standing. The pit below was dry, since the water was being kept out of there by coffer dams and diversion tunnels; but on either side of the coffer dams I could see the Sutlej lying, its surface green and wrinkled in the sunshine. There were all kinds of things down in the pit — railways, mouths of tunnels, a couple of dozen little one-room shacks. But instead of dwelling on these objects I tried to visualize what the scene would be like when there was just one great mass of concrete between my location and theirs. It was a prodigious vision, and besides there would be a prodigious lake on the concrete's upstream side — three hundred and sixty-six villages would be submerged by it, I understood. Nehru had been right, I felt, in calling the

job tremendous, stupendous and something which shakes
you up.

About eight thousand Indians are employed at Bhakra,
of whom two thousand are clerks. Slocum thinks both
these figures are too high, and the second one is especially so. He says that in America he would have no
more than five hundred clerks on such a job, and he
might get them down to three hundred. In truth he seems
to be up against some rules of Asian society that he cannot change and that differ from what he is used to. One
of these rules is that a job should feed as many mouths
as it can, most of them on a level of bare subsistence. Another is that educated men should not work with their
hands. A third, apparently, is that action can rarely be
taken unless a paper scheme for it has been worked out
beforehand. Slocum complains that he can't simply appear somewhere on the job and tell the men there to
build something that needs building — a drain or retaining wall, for instance — as he might in America. Instead
he must return to the administration building and get
someone there to draw a plan of what he wants, following which the laborers can be activated. "The paper takes
longer than the actual work," he says, "but they've got
to do it that way." Indian engineers lean to the academic,
rather than the practical, in their training and outlook,
and Slocum dislikes this — partly, of course, because he
has had so little academic training himself. "The engineer here is so immersed in his paper work that he has no

time to do his engineering," Slocum complains. "He becomes more of a bookkeeper than he is an engineer or an executive. He gets stuck with what the book said when he went to college, and he can't get beyond this. That's not my way. I see it fresh and I see it deep." Slocum is especially ill broken to office routine, perhaps — he told me once during my visit that he had never dictated a letter in his life, but instead had just written in longhand or had scribbled down notes for a secretary to copy. Even allowing for this idiosyncrasy, though, he seems to have grounds for some complaint. The class distinction of being a white-collar man is so highly prized by educated Indians, as by other educated Asians, that they often refuse to spoil it by indulging in action. This inhibits the Indian supervisory staff at Bhakra from behaving as an American staff would — from scrambling round the hillsides, that is, getting dirty, and showing the workmen how to do things. Slocum says the situation has changed a lot since he came, and that he has driven or shamed much of the staff to go out on the job now (and also to remove their neckties, which is symbolic of conversion to his outlook). But the fact remains that Indian engineers are, by definition, men of repose rather than action. When an Indian engineer at Bhakra has a car assigned to him, Slocum says, he immediately has a driver assigned too, and the latter thenceforth attends to things like servicing — tasks that in Slocum's eyes are an integral part of the construction man's estate. The Indian engineers also have chuprassies, or personal office servants, assigned to them. As is customary in India, the chuprassies wear elaborate liveries that include things like yellow turbans and long scarlet coats. They look strange indeed in the Bhakra administration buildings, whose interior decoration is in the American-engineering style — rooms of wallboard and raw concrete, that is, lit starkly by fluorescent lights. The presence of the drivers and chuprassies helps to underline their principals' high status, and that is one reason for having them on the job. Another is to feed that many more poor Indians who have some claim on someone connected with the project — to feed them not handsomely, but enough to live on. This made-work attitude to the job was everywhere when Slocum arrived, though he says he has overcome it somewhat. The Bhakra trucks carry only drivers now, for instance, instead of drivers and "sweepers" — or drivers' helpers — as they used to. Again, hand shovels at Bhakra are no longer managed by two men — one of them pulling a rope attached to the handle near the blade — as formerly. While cutting down the number of laborers Slocum has also tried to raise their comfort standard, and with it their efficiency, by transporting them to work, for instance, and supplying them with drinking water at their posts — favors that were not thought necessary before. He cites these changes as progress, but not as victory. He is working with an unfamiliar social structure, where the individual ranks low and caste ranks high. He realizes this, though he is not reconciled to it. He fights it while fighting the problems of nature.

The complaints at Bhakra are not all on Slocum's side, it should be said. He has an American staff of thirty-odd men helping him boss the job, and a great many Indians feel that these men are too many, are too highly paid, and are objectionable in other ways too. I did not probe these Indian complaints deeply during my visit, but I picked up some knowledge of them in passing. An Indian engineer told me that the highest annual salary drawn by any of his countrymen at Bhakra was forty thousand rupees, or between eight and nine thousand dollars (he omitted to mention various perquisites, however, such as a house, car, driver and chuprassy, which would bring the job's value up several thousand rupees more). He said that many of the Americans, by contrast, drew more than a hundred thousand rupees a year, especially if one counted the income taxes that were forgiven them by the Indian Government under their contracts. I didn't check these figures in detail, but I think the general burden of them was true. Our American living standard is so high that American technicians will rarely come to Asia unless promised two or three times as much pay as their Asian counterparts. This is an accepted rule of the relationship, and my Indian informant was not really objecting to it. His point, rather, was that there were too many Americans on the job, and that this was costing his country foreign exchange that she could ill spare. He said that nowhere else in India was there such a concentration of Americans on any project. He said there was much criticism of this in the neighborhood, and that some ignorant Indians — those not in a position to see what the Americans were doing — felt that ninety per cent of them should be sent home. Others felt that eighty per cent should go, according to my informant; and the average, charitable view (to which he sub-scribed) was that fifty per cent should. He felt there was reason to hire expensive Americans if the job would be done more quickly thereby, but that few of the Americans at Bhakra actually qualified on this count, and that otherwise their only justification was their value as trainers — many of them were specialists in certain machines and techniques, and he felt they should be kept on the job long enough, and only long enough, to impart their knowledge to some Indian pupils.

Though my informant was reserved on the point, I also sensed that behind the Indian resentment of the Americans' expensiveness was a certain resentment of their manner — that some Americans, anyway, were tactlessly given to showing their scorn of Indian methods, and even to suggesting that the Indian engineers didn't have a proper spirit about the job (since they were reluctant, for instance, to dirty their hands on it). Again I didn't go into the details, but I believe there was justification for this Indian feeling. Slocum agreed in fact, to some extent, in that he felt certain Americans coming to the job had been temperamentally unqualified for it. He said he had never been able to forecast how Americans would turn out on these overseas jobs. "Most Americans shouldn't be given passports even to visit a foreign country," he remarked. "On a job like this we are down-to-earth ambassadors or envoys of the United States. But some men come out here and get frustrated and exasperated because they can't get things done in the U.S. way. Then they go to hell in a handbasket." This failing was, of course, one more of Slocum's problems.

Slocum's own value to the job was not doubted by the Indians, I gathered in my cursory study of their opinion. He was somewhat criticized for being harsh, and especially for blowing up at Indian engineers and destroying their face when other Americans were present — a grave offense anywhere in the East. I felt sure that his hard-driving tactics made his Indian subordinates uncomfortable, no matter how much they respected him. I also gathered that they held him in great awe and had virtually no feeling of intimacy toward him. He didn't encourage such a feeling. While driving above the dam site he would give lifts to Indian employees whom we passed, and he also carried a bag of hard candies that he would distribute to children by the roadside now and then. These gestures were made in an openhanded, friendly spirit, I felt, but they did not lessen Slocum's lonely attitude to the job. He ruled out personal attachments with anyone on it.

Slocum's relationship with Nehru appears to be quite good. Nehru has a way of developing informal friendships with key people, including foreigners, who are important to India. Through these ties he can keep in touch with the other parties and co-operate with them.

Thus he can advance projects that might otherwise be blocked by red tape. He met Slocum at a Bhakra reception in 1953, and took him aside there and told him he must drop in to call whenever he visited New Delhi. Slocum has made a habit of this. Aside from the pleasure he takes in these calls they enable him to get the heat applied to some of his administrative and supply problems. Sometimes he takes such problems up with Nehru directly, but often he doesn't have to because his mere access to the great man keeps the rest of the officialdom alert to help him. Slocum thinks his Indian colleagues would like to do the right thing by him, but that often they can't. When first he arrived on the job, in the spring of 1952, he had a series of talks with Indian officials in which they promised him many things that they could not later fulfill. He thinks now that they were frightened of him and didn't dare say no, but at the time he thought they had the power. "I thought in the beginning that this thing was so important to them that they would waive anything," he remarked to me, "because it was a battle. But now I've found that it's impossible for them to move on some things." One thing they can't move on easily is the procurement of supplies, which is naturally hedged about with bureaucratic restrictions, and which in Bhakra's case is further inhibited by the fact that before Slocum's coming a huge mass of American Army surplus, from World War II, had been bought for Bhakra with the idea — then prevalent in many parts of the world — that this would be a cheap way to become well equipped mechanically. Instead most of the surplus turned out to be ill suited to the job, and it has spent the intervening years rusting in the Nangal yards. Slocum would like to sell it as scrap, he says, but cannot, in many cases, because this would formalize the loss and would require that someone get blamed for negligence in the original purchase — the kind of outcome that is avoided in bureaucratic setups everywhere. Slocum showed me virtual acres of useless equipment — a lot of rusty winches, for instance, that would have to go on rusting because they might bring only ten dollars each as scrap whereas they were on the books at about seventy dollars. This was one of Slocum's man-made obstacles. Others included mistakes that had been committed before he came on the scene — such as the location of the two workers' villages, already mentioned, in a place where they would be submerged as the water rose behind the dam. Slocum said he would soon have to move these villages or reduce his labor force, and he considered this to be a needless affliction. He was fighting such things. In a way he was fighting some of India's more primitive aspects, and in this it was useful to have the help of Nehru, who is an old hand at fighting them himself.

In the evenings I would sit in Slocum's little house and listen to him. He lived simply, and he said this was the first time he had had a servant on any job. The servant in question, a Bengali cook-bearer who spoke fair English, seemed rather puzzled by Slocum but not overworked by him. There was an electric refrigerator in the dining room, and some time before lunch or dinner Slocum would look into this, and into a cupboard of canned foods, and would order impromptu snacks for himself and me, according to our tastes. If he didn't finish his snack he would have it kept and reheated for the next meal. He didn't seem to care much what he ate, and I believe this was a disappointment to the servant, who had little chance to show his talent. Slocum also took a small assortment of "stay-alive" pills at meals — precautions against coronary occlusions, from which he suffers. Before and after each meal we would sit in his bedroom, where he kept a desk, a simple high bed, like a hospital bed, and a couple of fairly severe chairs. He would sit up straight in one of the chairs and talk. The house had a living room, with a conventional set of armchairs and sofa, but Slocum used this only to receive callers. The bedroom was rather like a hermit's cell, and I think it suited him to spend his time in such a place, with his books and papers close at hand. He told me he had thought of having a little hut built for himself near the top of the gorge, above the dam site, where he could keep an eye on the job. Had he done this, he said, he would like to have secretly installed some "telltales" in the hut — electric lights wired to flash on if the machinery shut down anywhere, thus enabling him to appear swiftly and mysteriously at the spot in question. He liked the idea of being thought omniscient by his subordinates. He said he often went to sleep with his lights on — dozing off while reading in bed — and that on some jobs this had had the desirable effect of not letting people know when he actually slept, if ever.

He talked to me a good deal about water, or hydraulics, a field to which he had given much thought. "The entire history of man," he said once, "is tied to what he has done, and what he is doing, with the available supply of water. You can't do a damn thing without water, and you can't produce more water than falls. Therefore you must conserve it." He felt that man had been criminal in his misuse of the water supply. "In the food-gathering age man didn't use more than two gallons of water a day," he said. "But now in the U.S. probably more than fifteen hundred gallons are used per day per person. Mostly this is because of industrialization. It takes sixty-five thousand gallons of water to make a ton of steel, and three hundred thousand to make a ton of aluminum." Warming to his lecture, Slocum explained that the great civilizations had all sprung up in river valleys, but in time these had become overpopulated in relation to the water supply. "Then you got irrigation," he said. "First you got diversion dams and canals. Then people discovered that dams could be used for storage. Then for flood control. Then for electricity — that was in the late 1880s, the earliest hydroelectric development. It was found that dams could also be used for navigation and for recreation, of course. Nowadays every big dam has most of these uses, perhaps all six of them." Slocum paused awhile and thought, sitting relaxed and comfortable, though erect. In these discourses he was quiet and cozy, but still zestful (his speech was seasoned with a fair amount of obscenity that is omitted here). "Yes," he said, "man's future is tied irrevocably to what he does with the water. With proper control of water the earth might support ten billion people — it is now supporting two and a half billion. Man is going to use up his easy supplies of metal, and he will use up his fuels. He will find substitutes for these things, but not for the water." I asked him about sea-water recovery, and he said the expense was prohibitive, and would be for a long time. He did mention some variable factors in the water supply, though, one being the size of the polar icecaps. "You have much less water in circulation during an ice age," he said, "because so much of it is frozen." He thought the water table — the level of underground water — was an important thing too, and a tricky one. "Here in India the water table is high, thank God, because the Persian wheels they use in their wells can't draw from very far down. But they are putting in tubewells now, with electric power, and that will lower the table. They should be very careful. If the fresh-water table goes too low, then salt water will come in and they will have trouble. That's what happened in California." He denounced overgrazing, too, as an artificial way of decreasing the water supply, by hastening runoff.

Slocum had a close knowledge of the world's rivers. He told me that the biggest river, in volume of flow, was the Amazon, which put out seven million two hundred thousand second-feet, or cusecs, a day. The next biggest was the Paraná-Río de la Plata, also in South America, and the next was the Congo. All these rivers were difficult, if not impossible, to dam in their lower reaches because they flowed through swamps or soft alluvial plains. The fourth biggest river, the Yangtze, was a different matter, though. It flowed through gorges and could be dammed beautifully — Slocum would love to work on the job. The fifth largest river, he said, was the combined Ganges and Brahmaputra in North India. The sixth was the Mekong in Southeast Asia (if it was not the Ob or the Yenisei, that is). The seventh was the Mississippi. Then came the Nile, the Volga, the Danube, the Indus and the Columbia, in that order. Slocum explained to me — something I hadn't realized — that you never got big rivers in small countries, like England or Japan, for instance, because the catchment areas were not extensive enough. Nor did you get really big rivers in steep mountains, because the valleys were too short there. The Sierra Nevada Range in California, for instance, had big mountains in it, but they didn't produce exceptionally big rivers. You needed something expansive and gradual, like the Mississippi Valley. Slocum ran on about these things, as if he were Old Man River himself. He touched on riparian rights — personal or national claims to water supply — as a hindrance to river development. He said this could be a serious problem. "The Danube, for instance, would make a wonderful river for development," he explained, "but they can't do a God-damn thing with it because it

runs through so God-damn many countries." He felt
that American river development was somewhat inhibited
by riparian rights, but not much — after all, we had
achieved some very big interstate projects. Of American
regions, he thought the Mississippi Valley had the greatest undeveloped water supply and therefore the greatest
room for population increase, though this was not being
used now because people didn't like to live there so well
as on the seaboards. He thought that New York and Los
Angeles had the worst water problems in America —
New York would soon have to be damming every little
stream in its hinterland, he said, and treating its sewage
water for re-use in industry. California would have to
do the same. "Every stream in California will be dammed
if possible," he said. "Then every one in the United
States. Then in the world." He discoursed on other hydraulic topics, like the probable reasons for the Sahara
and Gobi Deserts. Nor did he leave the subject when
we were out driving. In explaining about the heavy rains
of the year before — officially called the worst in a hundred years — he said he didn't know if these records were
correct or not, but he could guarantee that the rains had
been the worst in the life of the present vegetation. He
pointed out innumerable new sandy scars in the brush
of the hills, where there had been small landslides. No
other great downpour could have happened, he maintained, since that particular brush had been in place, or
there would be many ancient scars in addition to the new
ones. He had long practiced reading the banks and hill-

sides this way, he said. Once in Alaska, during the war, he had advised an American general not to park some equipment for the winter at a certain place beside the Yukon. The general had disregarded his advice, and by spring the equipment had all been buried under ice cakes. Slocum said scars on the bank gave clear warning that this would happen. Such river lore seemed always to be with him as he surveyed the Sutlej. The Sutlej was running at about four thousand second-feet a day while I was there. In May, when the snows would be melting in earnest, it might get up to fifty thousand second-feet. And in the summer monsoons two hundred thousand, or even three hundred and fifty thousand, was the expected volume. But it might be more than this. Engineers had a hypothetical maximum flow for any given river, which they called the "thousand-year flood." Slocum had to be ready for a thousand-year flood on the Sutlej any summer, and against such a possibility he had to keep close watch on the river's behavior.

He philosophized to me about nonhydraulic things too, including the subject of thought itself. "Man hates to use his brain," he said to me one evening. "He likes only to use his mouth and his [something not mentionable in print]. I am not talking about the *un*favored few who are natural thinkers. They're thinking all the time, wondering about the reasons for what they see. They can't help it." I believe Slocum counted himself among the few who were given to thinking (and it is a classification that

I would second). "I have only one rule," he told me once, "and that is 'To thine own self be true.' You've got to say to yourself: 'You stupid son of a bitch, why did you do that?' And then change." He felt that bureaucratic thinkers could never be original because they disregarded this rule and aimed instead at "security," a goal he was inevitably scornful of. "Security was the downfall of the Romans, Egyptians and all of them," he said. "Yes, and the British, and it's going to be the downfall of us too." He liked to make short generalizations — almost aphorisms, they were — about life. He had a set of three words — "organize, deputize and supervise" — which between them could describe, he felt, all mankind's efforts at leadership. He also thought that most of man's endeavors could be reduced to the question of movement. "I've always said," he explained, "that broadly everything man does is a problem in transportation. To build a dam, for instance, you need roads on which to move the dirt out, to bring the cement in, and so forth. If you are a farmer you plow the field — the animal has to move the plow. You cut the grain, which is a problem of transporting the blade to the stalks. Then you haul the result off to the mill." He turned to me and got more personal. "For you to do an article," he said, "you must go somewhere and get the information. Then you must transport it to the magazine, which in turn transports it to the readers. All movement, you see."

In regard to American politics Slocum was a conservative or reactionary. He was against Franklin Roosevelt, against the TVA, against strong unions. He was frankly a rugged individualist, and against anything that might limit his sovereignty as such. One evening I asked him about the Russians, and whether he thought they could swing a job like Bhakra. He said they could, but not with economy and speed, because they used European equipment, and this was too small. "I call European machines 'tinker toys,' " he said. "No one else makes such good stuff as the United States. This means right down to wire rope. It is because we have the habit of getting the bugs out all the time, by trial and error. In Europe the manufacturer thinks that what he builds is good enough, and he doesn't listen to the customer, but in America the customer can get any changes he wants." I asked Slocum if there were any exceptions to his rule of American superiority, and he said no. "We make better God-damn things than anybody else makes period," he said. "I buy Swiss watches, because that is the fashion, but in America we make just as good watches as anyone. We've made more automobiles in one year than all the rest of the world. A part that you get from us to put in an automobile fits because it's been made on a jig that can't make anything else. In Europe they make them on lathes with a micrometer, and the output varies." Slocum said that in thirty years the Russians had increased their steel capacity by ten times, but he didn't think their quality was up to ours, or that they had achieved anything like our degree of automation. He felt they were trying to copy us as the Japanese had, but they didn't put into it what we did. He related this failing to their lack of the competitive system, in which he felt their country must be rather like India. "When I have a rail shipment coming from Bombay," he said, "I regularly have someone ride in the car. If I don't do this it takes a hundred and twenty days to get here — ten miles a day — and I never know where the shipment is. In America you can find out where a freight car is every day, and that is because of the competitive system. I think Russia must be like India in this respect, because she has no competitive system either." I cannot judge the correctness of these remarks by Slocum, and I repeat them because they help to round out the picture of him, not because they necessarily describe the world's true state. Slocum was so original, I felt, that he did not have to be right always — he could afford to be wrong, or at least questionable, for the sake of riding his own line. He certainly didn't have to be consistent. Despite his simple life at Bhakra he told me he had enough good suits at home to go for thirty or thirty-five days without wearing the same one twice, and he had a fine wardrobe in all respects. "I like all that," he said. "I like the feel of the good shirts." And despite his meager schooling, and his dislike of paper work, he was a voracious and catholic reader. His room had a big collection of books, mainly paperbound, including good fiction, common thrillers, and much nonfiction in science, history, religion and philosophy. He read incessantly in these, he said, and he appropriated their ideas in his own way. "I'm pretty much of a freethinker," he told me. "I make up my own mind about things." And that seemed one of the truest statements I heard all week end.

The Himalayas, where Slocum is now working, are original too. They are full of strange characteristics, strange legends, strange holy men who come and go with almost no possessions ("That's the life for me," Slocum said one day when we passed an especially light-traveling holy man on the road). The dam site itself has odd little shrines near it, and the place seems to be thought an auspicious one. Slocum's own strangeness seems to fit in well with the mountains. The rather superstitious peasants there are said to have great respect for him. Some have tried to give him land, some have come and waited twenty-four hours for a sight of him, and some believe — or so I was told — that he can see two hundred feet into the ground. When Bhakra is finished and Slocum is physically gone, therefore, one supposes that his spirit may linger in the legends of the place, quite at home. The dam itself will be his monument, and the echoes of his personality will doubtless hover round it.

A Nostalgia for Camels

I HAVE a friend, a scholar from deep Central Asia, from a people of Turkish culture. He doesn't like to be named, or described pointedly — wariness and discretion being prime traits of Central Asians, who have undergone bloody factional violence through all history. I can only say he has huge brown eyes that seem almost to pop from his head. When I first met him, at lunch in Peking, we sat opposite each other at a round table, and through the meal I had an urge to stretch a cupped hand toward him as a fireman's net for his eyes if they should leap. His eyes are expressive and so is his voice, which is resonant and can deal out a vigorous terse English of exotic sound and form.

He is a refugee from the brown sandstorm country of Marco Polo's silk route — now mainly in Red hands — and for the past phase he has lived in British Hong Kong, a green isle lapped by waves and doused in fogs and monsoons. He has seemed to me uneasy in this setting, a fish in Your Eyes," but we didn't go farther on that byway.

"These *buta* eyes," he said, "they are smoky. These *buta* eyes are not clear, not clear-looking, but they are smoky. With plenty of meaning. Lots of wish-meaning. When you look at them you can never answer." With his own smoky brown eyes, melodramatically, he gave a look that might be described as plaintive, beseeching, lonely. "They look at you," he said. "They want something, but you can never answer them, you know. Because they are animals." He gave the look again.

"But I tell you one thing," he continued. "No Hollywood actress if she had seen these *buta* eyes — she will surrender at once. Never mind what he or she is. If you see the *buta* eyes you will surrender yourself. Of *course* you will surrender. I am sure Gloria Swanson will surrender." He said Gloria Zwannzon. There was, of course no suggestion of a romance with a camel. It was simply that Miss Swanson or anyone else would give up all claim to expressive eyes after seeing those of a *buta*.

My friend had broken into a Central Asiatic song, and the interview was getting becalmed again.

I asked him when camels grew mature enough to reproduce, and this led to a long and tricky stretch of talk. I think we were both getting dreamy with the stout after our lunch. I don't know what my friend thought I was getting at now, but I know he was uneasy. When I asked a question he would look at me apprehensively or incredulously with his big brown eyes, and then give an

oblique answer. He seemed to need all the forbearance at
his disposal, and luckily there was a good deal. He is a
devout Muslim (if not too strict a keeper of all the rules),
and like many Muslims he feels a bond with Christianity.
He can be closer to an American than to a Chinese, for
instance, especially if the American shows respect for the
Church. So in a mood compounded of Guinness, generosity, distrust and religious fellowship he went on to tell
me about the mating habits of camels and how they are
controlled by caravan drivers, breeders and the like. He
said among other things that drivers — anxious to keep
their caravans moving — try to shorten the mating season
of male camels by tying their tails forward to their humps
or packsaddles, which is supposed to have a calming effect. The tying is done with strings of camel's-hair wool.

When this topic gave out I asked what camels were
called after their three-year-old, or *tailak*, period —
which, incidentally, he had told me was the age of ma-
turity.

"*Duye*," he said. "*Duye* is general name — means
camel. They are called this for the rest of their life, and
they live to be about thirty." He was getting off on his
own steam again. "You can go with them," he said.
"After three or four years of age you can ride camel
wherever you go." He seemed to have forgotten me.
"They never think," he said. "Never go crazy. This is
the best people in the world to engage with. These people — these camels — they will never betray you. They

will always faithful for you. I don't know why they are such people but they do it."

I had sometimes heard that camels had a mean streak. Long ago, in some dim adventure story, I had read of a camel's biting a man's kneecap off for spite — the kneecap of a Senegalese, perhaps — I couldn't remember. I asked my friend about this.

"There was no such case that they don't like you," he answered, and his voice rang. "Impossible. I have seen such cases of people writing that camels don't like you, and they spit on you. But it was not right."

I had slowed him down again. He sat there humming "Smoke Gets in Your Eyes" abstractedly. I asked him to tell me about the likes and dislikes of camels.

"They don't have any particular liking, you know," he said. "They go on, and they don't have anything. For three months is mating season. Other nine months they don't have anything they care about."

He was stalled again, humming.

I asked him about the care of camels' feet on long caravan trips, a problem I was sure had many angles to it. He didn't answer this time. He looked at me with his eyes, and excused himself to go to the bathroom.

He was gone a long time, and when I was beginning to worry about this I heard a cry, almost a sob, from his direction. I hurried there — it was down a corridor. My friend was standing in the middle of the room, pointing downward and to one side, a look of dismay on his face.

"You *can't*," he said.

I looked where he was pointing, and it was at a legend on the toilet seat. "Church Seat," it said, "Regal, Sheet Covered," whatever that meant. I gathered that a manufacturer named Church had turned it out.

"You *can't*," my friend said in agitation. "Church is holy place. You can't do this thing."

I told him I was sorry, and the seat would be gone to-morrow. I led him to the next room and sat down with him, and we talked of general things. After a while he was composed and took his leave.

That was the end of my research in camel nostalgia, and I am no nearer to plumbing the secrets of Asia or of exile.